# FRESH PERSPECTIVES ON FICTION

# FRESH PERSPECTIVES ON FICTION

Mulk Raj Anand, R.K. Narayan
and Raja Rao

*By*
**Suresh Chandra**

**ANMOL PUBLICATIONS PVT. LTD.**
**NEW DELHI - 110 002 (INDIA)**

**ANMOL PUBLICATIONS PVT. LTD.**
4374/4B, Ansari Road, Daryaganj
New Delhi - 110 002
Ph.: 23261597, 23278000
Visit us at: www.anmolpublications.com

*Fresh Perspectives on Fiction*



First Published, 2005

ISBN 81-261-2126-2



PRINTED IN INDIA

---

**Published by J.L. Kumar for Anmol Publications Pvt. Ltd., New Delhi - 110 002 and Printed at Mehra Offset Press, Delhi.**

# Contents

# Introduction

Indian attempts to create literature in English date back to 1864 when Bankim Chandra Chatterjee published his novel *Rajmohan's Wife* in that year. It does not mean, however, that literary activity before that period was non-existent in India. Much before the novel came into being in the West, India had a highly developed tradition of literary expression that gave us excellent works of art like *Jatak Kathas, Panchatantra, Hitopadesh, Dashkumar Charita*. The Mughals brought with them an excellent tradition of story telling. It is evident in the widely circulated stories of Hatim Tai, Alibaba and Forty Thieves, Kissa Tota-Maina ad infinitum collectively known as *Arabian Nights*. Fiction in India was, thus, known much before the arrival of Balzac, Hugo, Scott and Dickens on the Western horizon who chaperoned the infant art of fiction writing in the West by setting norms and investing dimensions to it. In a way it could be said that the art of fiction writing in the West was in a way a sort of re-invention after the Dark Ages in the history of mankind. The Indian works, which were timeless in setting and which transcended all the superficial barriers had simply gone under the cover of darkness extending over intervening ages.

The fateful eighteen fifties saw the triumph of the West over India. The defeat of nationalist forces on the political and military fronts in 1857 crushed the national spirit and allowed free sway to English culture, language, religion and taste over those Indian. The upper crust that had the privilege of indulging learning and knowledge as a pastime, was the first to respond to the changed situation in which English would be the masters for a long time to come. There was no better way to demonstrate this shift in outlook than to adopt English looks that would establish the link between the aristocrat, as the middle man and the distanced master. It is wrong to say, as has become the fashion among Indian literary historians and critics, that English was thrust on Indians by Macaulay. Much before Macaulay was born, English had been a medium not of official communication alone but had begun to be used for literary expression too, an activity thoroughly voluntary, as evidenced in Raja Ram Mohan Roy's efforts to popularise English in India. It could be more meaningful if done through the vernacular. The very fact that literature, as the expression for abstracted privatized feeling and experience, is offered for sharing by the public at large, is sufficient to explode the myth that seeks to justify, nay glorify, the attempts of all those Indians who opted to write literature in English. No Englishman, in his arrogance of pride and essential humility, would care to read and not many Indians would be sufficiently equipped and interested in benefiting from such an exercise. For whom was it written, then? Obviously, for the consumption of a small circle of family and friends and the satisfaction of the vanity of the self. Nobody read their works those days for the simple reason of the widespread illiteracy as well as the lack of enthusiasm and social discouragement to learn English. Nobody reads them today except an antiquarian and an academician interested in the history of the genre in India. These works discourage the reader for their narrow sweep and their indifference to the vital issues affecting the masses. This may be due to the changed circumstances under which the Victorianism looks archaic, hence bemusing. Devoid of the knowledge of life at any other level except their own—a sad commentary on the existence of the upper crust of society that lives and dies for the self and refuses to know the rest. This draws upon only on the romantic past woven around the traits of feudalism including their escapades. The writers did not have to depend upon the patronage of the buyer masses those days because the masses neither had the equipment nor the time to invest in reading. The wealthy had all the leisure and means and also the desire to establish himself as an intellectual. So he published himself supported by sychophants as to the merits of his work and also burning with a desire to appear as an intellectual. All those who believe in the Macaulay myth may be aware that India has been a land not so much of promise as that of opportunism. If anything thrives here, it is opportunism that seeks to thrive at the misery of the other—a cut throat existence in which the nearer and the dearer is mostly the object of contempt, of derision and of little importance—an unsuspecting prey that could be sacrificed at convenience. This typical Indian mentality and conduct has smeared the whole record of the race over millennia and the history is replete with incidents when one would not reconcile to minor lapses on the part of one's fellowman but would prefer, to build fortunes instead, by subserving the interests of any unknown devil in order to exterminate the known affliction. The Indian continues to be both accommodative and tolerant of others and un-accommodative and violently intolerant of one's fellowman, both at the same time, thus winning laurels from all the distant corners to the woe of the neighbour next door. This attitude alone could be held responsible for the Indian's looking to the West — its life-styles, its language, its culture and his more than willingness to accept whatever could be used as a pretext for unbridled freedom and rejecting whatever could not be subservient to his narrow outlook and base needs. We (continue life styles) to welcome ideas and visions from the west in contempt of indigenous achievements. We acclaim, however, our own attainments only after recognition flows from abroad. We imitate their life-styles without caring to understand their compulsions; their language and speech without appreciating the cultural reinforcement that is too demanding and inflexible; their acts without caring to comprehend their total outlooks. However, we implant and imprint and keep grumbling when the results are not to our expectation. Notwithstanding the volume of criticism produced over ages, we continue to behave as we do for no criticism works except a cut on the self. But that is always an isolated event. The lack of fellow feeling, the lack of intention to think of the self as a part of the whole rather the whole made of the self continues to dictate our priorities. It is the result of this continuum that we have a vast body of literature in Indolish—a tradition that began before the first decade of the vanquishing of Indian national honour and aspiration was over. There may be an objection to whatever has been said above because of the whole philosophy of '*Vasudhaiv kutumbakam*' that has shaped the psyche of the perennial Indian. It needs to be understood that our achievements in the ancient past are not being lost sight of. Those were the ideal times when the landscape was dotted by fewer individuals and the resources were in excess of the demands. With the increasing number of claimants and the corresponding shrinkage of opportunity the various vices are bred. The cut-throat competition for space and means compells the weaker to be meaner too. However, the prolonged suppression of a large section by a minuscule section and the cruel denial of the right to live with the minimum human dignity and their sudden awakening and acquiring strength to fight injustice has turned tables the world over. The old order, however good it was, has tumbled and a so called chaos prevails because of the claim of the masses on the fruit of labour and endeavour. A new kind of thinking is in the air and a new kind of humanism too that does not subsist on the mercy of enlightened classes because it puts forth its own claim to enlightenment and its capability to attain that. Thus, the old myths of genetic or inherent superiority and status based on these hackneyed notions have started exploding and, for the good of mankind too.

Literary activity is as much a part of politics as the game of politics itself. No writer remains uninformed of the political developments that could affect him and his people and, in consequence, informs the politics of the needs and sentiments of his subjects. No aspect of human nature and activity remains affected by politics and vice-versa. It is conspicuous by its absence in the concerns of the writers of the age at a time when so much was happening within and without the country. Instead, we find our early writers beginning with translations from English and taking up themes, thereafter, depicting aspects of Indian life that hardly do any credit to the artist. Most of the early novels deal with the seduction of charming girls by wealthy persons. The primary reason behind the selection of such themes could be afflictions like misery, ostracism, casteism, exploitation etc. These were beyond the comprehension and the total experience of the creative writers of the nineteenth century who preferred to look at these with indulgence. Their primary motive was to impress the British public with their command over the English language rather than to acquaint them with the political or social situation obtaining at home at the time.

The First World War, however, seems to have shaken the world not only politically but socially too. The whole outlook undergoes a change. The common man becomes the point of focus and his plight invites the attention of the intellectual more than the life at the royal court or the harem. The industrial revolution in printing and transport prove a boon for the humanity at the lower rung because his cooperation becomes indispensable. He assumes more importance not only as the operator of the machine but also as the consumer of its product. The rise of the merchant class as the new controller of man and material steals the limelight from the traditional wealthy. Consequently, Indolish writers' perception is affected too. Earlier he wrote for the self-glorification. Now he adopts it as a vocation. English offers a lucrative market for him since a book written in English would sell in all the corners of the world. Besides, recognition abroad has always been considered a sure recommendation for recognition at home. The peculiar Indian tendency is to downgrade the compatriot and delight in suppressing and marring the other's talent with a Dostoeveskian non-chalant tongue-in-cheek manner. Anything, therefore, from the foreign shores is fit only to be set in the crown. Many an Indian talent has suffered because of this oriental complex. The moment the West sees some talent and quality in somebody or something, we start seeing too much thereafter and not before. Kalidas, Khayyam and Tagore would have remained just ordinary poets if the West had not seen beauty par excellence in their works. Shakespeare, on the other hand, continues to be a great poet, merely because the recognition comes from the West and not because we discover virtue in him. The Indian writer's first priority remains therefore, to do something to arrest the imagination not of the people around but of the distantly placed. His decision to write in English, to begin with, is primarily aimed at being known farther. This contention is further supported by the fact that the Indian sub-continent is divided into more than a score of linguistic zones exclusivity dominated by well developed languages and rich cultural and literary traditions. The situation is further complicated with the Indian's conscious refusal to recognise any other Indian language as a ligua franca. This, however, is a grotesque situation: a common medium of communication means a free pass for entering a culture-house at will and be a privy to its secrets and possessions. It also facilitates misuse and distortions by way of the contribution of the common pool user of the medium. Now, if the common medium of expression also happens to be the first language of a community or section, the integral cultural life of its native speaker becomes a common property too, taking away from him his privacy and exclusivity. It is ridiculous, therefore for any language-speaking community to campaign for the status of lingua franca to its language. It is as good as making one's language a common whore parading the streets naked for anyone and everyone to see, abuse its charms without obligation to defend its honour and fend for its needs. The widespread use of English in a large part of the globe is a glaring testimony to the above observation—everyone renders his thoughts in English without being aware how many scars he has caused on its white skin. The White English, the Black English, the Brown English, the Yellow English, the Yankee English—as if the Clown English were to appear in different garbs to entertain different pay-masters in different shows. This is no better than the cross-bred bastard varieties of English. In India, English is used for communication with diverse linguistic regions too.

A language away from its geography, culture and social environment tends to shed its core features of intonation, semantic as well as syntactic. Its lexicon too is affected to a very large extent. All these modifications make it an entirely new entity so much as to make it a different language while retaining the essential links with the parent language. This is how all the languages are born and the present day English in India as a separate language is no exception to the above rule. Over the years it has acquired Indian regional characteristics and is no longer the language of the native of England. The strongest footing on which a language can claim an identity is the availability of literature in it. In this respect too Indolish is not found wanting since a vast body of literature in the form of prose, fiction, poetry, drama and even philosophical expositions is available in it. It is wholly indigenous and is part of Indian culture with Indian setting, characters, situations and problems. References to Indian mythology dominate its themes and Indian social taboos, aspirations and typical Indian view of life affect its nuances. Literature in Indolish, thus, offers Indian perception of reality of life with its songs and sorrows.

Indian literature is distinguishable from the literature of the rest of the world chiefly by the shaping influence of the dream of Ram Rajya that has continued to seize and direct the conduct of an average Indian for ages. This abiding dream of Ram Rajya has been manifest not only in the writings but even in the day-to-day conduct of the people small and big, average and prominent alike. The average Indian dreams of the establishment of an order in which the weak and the mighty, the poor and the rich would jostle and thrive and share equal honour and distinction. The establishment of a just society in which the above-average would be required to be more meticulous in his conduct as a model for the teeming millions below has been a commonly desirable trait of Indians. Inspired by the example of Ram in renouncing Sita on an objection by a common washerman, our leaders and writers have always strived hard to emulate Rama. The rise of socialistic concern for the position of the down and out so as to strengthen the base of the welfare State, has however, caused upheaval in public opinion, of late. It has compelled public opinion to recognise the inherent injustice to Sita who is punished in spite of her proven innocence, penance and sincere devotion. The modern Indian woman is no longer a passive slave of convention, situation and mother Nature. She refuses to suffer in the image of Sita, Draupadi and Savitri. She has not forsaken her worldly domain and its corresponding demands. She is more decisive, determined and alert to her place, privilege and role. She does not hesitate to take up challenges. She is more assertive in addition to being traditionally introspective. So is the case with the poor and the down trodden. He does not wait for charity to come to him. He resolves to make a decisive move and demands everything as his due. Literary writing is now crowded with those faceless of yesterdays. They discourse and delight and draw tears too. All together it is new kind of writing for which English has been found to be a liberating medium. It is so because it does not enforce its code of form, ethics, subtleties and nuances upon its non-native users. English is a helpless maid at the pleasure of non-conformist masses. Indian creativity that reflects through English clothes is, thus unique in hue, charm and characteristics. It is evident in the writings of the first set of writers who have very interestingly carved out distinct territories for themselves, as if out of some secret understanding. The names that dominate the opening scene are those of Mulk Raj Anand, RK Narayan and Raja Rao.

# Mulk Raj Anand

Mulk Raj Anand, the doyen of Indolish novelists (1905-) born in Peshawar city of undivided India and the scene of important historical events was the son of a Hindu father and a sikh mother. His father Lal Chand was a kshatriya silversmith by caste and rose to be Head clerk of his Regiment - a position of great honour for any Indian of ordinary parentage and means in the British India of those days. His mother, Ishwar Kaur, came from a still humbler peasant family. Like any Indian woman she too was devout but worshipped Christ and Agha Khan too, besides Krishna and Guru Nanak. Though she became an object of ridicule within the family and apparently Mulkraj felt encouraged to be a sceptic, she influenced him by her love and was a great shaping force behind him. The untiring crusader against all irrationalities in man, particularly Indian, the writer Anand is largely influenced by the bad conditions that existed at home. He was too curious a child to be normally borne with by his father. Lal Chand had acquired considerable military stubbornness coupled with his zeal for his son to acquire merit for entry into the Sahebdom of the mighty British Indian government. However, the son started developing aversion to his father's too subservient an attitude to the government. The satyagraha and the non-violence propagated by Mahatma Gandhi as a means to attain Independence, was very much in the air and was catching on fast with the youth. The masses were feeling awakened. In the process, many hidden ugly facets of the Indian social setup too were being recognized as detrimental to the interests of the freedom movement. Anand, then, was at the stage of initiation in his life.

He obtained his B.A. (Hons.) as a student of Khalsa College, Amritsar. Here he made friendship with Noor Muhammad and also fell in love with Yasmin, his friend's sister-in-law. She was married to a railway guard but Mulk Raj and Yasmin continued to meet clandestinely, helped and abetted by Noor and his wife. Yasmin's husband, however, came to know of their affair and their plans to elope misfired. Yasmin died under mysterious circumstances. This proved a double shock to him. Faced with the wrath of his father besides the loss of his beloved, he decided to go to London for higher studies in Philosophy and wrote his Ph.D. thesis under the guidance of Professor Dawes Hicks.

In England, Anand met Irene, the daughter of a Science Professor and fell in love with her. She was so much infatuated with him that listening to the account of his Indian life Mulk Raj was writing in the form of a novel, she promised to type out the script and also to marry him if he could publish the book. But, as his luck would have it, he lost his love because he could not find a publisher for his book, although he was awarded a Ph.D. in 1932. Heart-broken, he fell in love with a theatre-actress Kathleen Van Gelder and married her in 1932. A girl named Rajani was born to them before he settled down in India. After his arrival in Bombay, his interests in arts made him much sought after, particularly by a hill-woman of great charms, Anil de Silva. He was so much enamoured of her beauty that he went to London to divorce Kathleen so that he could marry Anil de Silva in India. By the time Anand came back, however, Anil had already left for Paris after marrying a Frenchman. The shock of this realisation was nerve-wrecking on him. But, this time a Greek dancer Melpo nursed him back to health over a long period and suggested he write out his anguish in the form of a novel, later titled *Private Life of an Indian Prince.*

Anand's stay abroad was very rewarding. He says that it helped him understand India objectively and better. There he met and became intimate with several celebrities like critic Bonamy Dobree, philosopher Bertrand Russell, American novelist Gertrude Stein, poets T.S. Eliot, Dylan Thomas, Lowes Dickinson, Eric Gill, novelists E.M. Forster, Virginia Woolf, D.H. Lawrence and French poet Andre Breton, Italian intellectual Anthony M. Ludovici, Indians J. Krishnamurthy, V.K. Menon and Anand Coomarswamy and many others.

He returned to India in 1932 and stayed with Gandhiji at Sabarmati Ashram for some time. Here he showed the Mahatma the draft of his first novel. On suggestions of the greatman he rewrote the whole story recasting Bakha as we find him in *Untouchable*. In 1935, he represented India at the International Writers' Movement. In 1952 he was awarded International Peace Prize of the World Peace Council. He has also been Chairman of Lalit Kala Akademi. In 1967, he was honoured with the Padma Bhushan. He was awarded Sahitya Akademi Award for his novel *Morning Face* in 1972. He is also the founder editor of the prestigious art journal *Marg*.

*Keep these facts in Mind while studying the work of Mulk Raj Anand:*

Mulk Raj Anand belongs to Panjab. Jammu-Kashmir, Panjab, Rajasthan and Gujarat are the western border states of present India. For ages invaders from the west have been entering Indian mainland through these states. Among these Panjab frontier has been most vulnerable and focussed upon because of its fertile plains nourished by perennial water systems: Sindhu, Satlaj, Vyas, Jhelum and innumerable other mighty perennial streams. Extremely hot summers and chilly winters make men hardy, industrious but apprehensive of the stranger, because of the constant influx of people into the region. The Panjabi has to be, therefore, both brave, fierce, merciless and alert and an efficient manager of men material and lands and properties. These nerve wrecking compulsions make him loud mouthed, bonded to the like minded brethren but mean to the challenger. He is well built, confident of himself and cooperative within his circle of acquaintance. This has also made him contemptuous of those who are lower to him in wealth, complexion, social status because of his pride in being self-made and a descendent of bravemen. He is cunning vis-a-vis a rival and a martyr in a cause. He is highly emotional too because for him living in isolation is inconceivable. Because of millenia of defeats at the hands of the outsider coming from the west, he has developed a notion of the superiority of the fair-skin and somewhere in his heart of hearts he nurtures a desire to secure higher status by being higher on the lines of the victorious alien. This manifests in his love for alien language, mannerisms, behaviour, clothing as well his inclination to establish liasion with the superior alien not only to be closer to the mighty alien but also to be seen to be closer by others.

A cursory look at any of the characters of the novels of Anand will enlarge our understanding of its conduct in the light of the above observations. Bakha is aware of his weak social economic, political and academic position. He does not raise his objection anywhere. However, he is intelligent and realises that he can overcome his weaknesses by traversing the only path that could be opened: education. He stakes all his economic might—a few pice he has been able to hoard - to acquire this edge from the only feasible source of the son of the regimental babu. He does not resist or repulse any kind of man-handling, exploitation, denial and dispossession because he is not only in a hopeless minority but isolated within his own house. His father, younger brother and sister lack courage to support and fan the spark in him. They are all the product of a mould perfected over millenia. He realises, therefore, that his emancipation would come by breaking the stranglehold of tradition. This cannot however, happen by openly courting the option but only by a cunning device: lure the friendly son of the educated babu by the offer of money and receive from him the secret of learning. No elderly person would concede him this privilege.

The plight of Munoo, the Coolie, is slightly better. He is not 'untouchable'. He is allowed entry in the houses of the upper caste men and he can touch their utensils. However, his economic status is too low to attract any type of recognition. He is well built too. Youth is the enviable capital of all: poor - rich, educated - illiterate, low caste - upper caste. Munoo, therefore, allows his youth to be capitalised. He can think of no better options than lifting heavy loads in the grain-vegetable market, working in a pickle factory, pulling a rickshaw. Even Mrs. Mainwaring is guided by only the consideration of his youth. It is interesting to note here that Munoo does not show a desire to 'rise' in life. He would be content with any situation ensuring him subsistence. We are under the mistaken notion that society does not put value on talent and its possessors. It is the possessor who must put value on himself and insist upon proper exchange price. In most of the cases of pathetic exploitation of man by man, it is the possessor of talent who fails in demanding proper price rather than the buyer of the talent failing to pay. Education equips and empowers the individual to evaluate his worth. Munoo fails to recognise it because he comes from the hills. Hills in India have traditionally been the destination of the aged who must practise renunciation preparatory to final departure from the world. Hills are the abode of the hermits, saints and scholars who rise above the charms of materialism. The notion is, people should opt to lose themselves in the hills to seek isolation by distancing after having indulged materialism in the youthful years. Having enjoyed the world to the maximum, an individual should concentrate upon the life after this life. Indian tradition does not envisage the young going to the hills. The world, with its charms, vices, tricks and deceits, attractions and promises spread over the plains towns, cities and metropolis is a school fit for youth to learn. It is a good workshop where they may practise their craft to their heart's content. Having spent his learning period in the viceless serene hills, uncouth Munoo descends to the plains like an unpolished rustic, a wild beast unaware of the vily craftsman of the plain and is easily taken for a ride there. No one aligns with Munoo because he is unaware of the strategies to market himself.

Gangu of *Two Leaves and a Bud* is no better than Munoo. He is a typical Indian farmer who is always indebted to the moneylender, the landlord and the government. This is generally because of his large heartedness, spendings, quarrels borne out of his arrogance generated by good crop yields. He refuses to realise the virtues of unostentatious living by modifying the needs arising out of imitative conduct. The focus here, however, is upon the exploitation of labour and abuse of human dignity of the peasant by British plantation owners. The interesting aspect of Indian life is that he exploits his fellow compatriot to his heart's content and prides in being successful to do so. But when he lands himself in the clutches of others, he cries foul. Gangu, the north-west Indian peasant leaves for a promised heaven in Assam tea-plantation. He must have suffered exploitation at the hands of his landlord in his native Panjab. However, he decides to migrate to Assam, in the north-east on the promise of heaven and realises that he has been lured into a trap. Though the author's intention is to highlight the British highhandedness in exploiting and heaping indignities upon the Indian labour a big question mark emerges here — the Western Gangu's decision to migrate to the east is equally symbolical of the perennial shift of the west towards the east and the attraction of the east towards the west. Gangu is impelled to migrate by his over brimming self-confidence that he can make heaven anywhere. His betrayal by the middleman confirms the presence of a class in the Indian society which not only thrives on the misery of the fellow human but also relishes the sadistic pleasure borne out of a psyche of vengenance. Before one dispossess another, he nurtures covetousness for long. Kashmir is all hills, although heaven like - remote and removed from the mainstream plains. It is quiet, serene and unpolluted. Though alien raiders have been entering the valley, they have been mesmerised by its innocence and beauty. Maqbool, therefore, represents a defenceless society taken by surprise. But he rises to the call of the situation as any self-respecting individual would do. However, Ahmed Shah represents the enemy within - those who thrive at the misery of others. Maqbool Sherwani senses the danger and visualises the horrifying consequences of Pakistani raiders' adventure. Like a genuine hillman, his intellectual level is so high that he is capable of reasoning out issues rather than be bogged down in appeals based on emotion and communalism. He realises that the atrocities are being committed by Muslim raiders from across the border, upon Muslim residents in the name of Islam. He rejects the appeal.

The plight of Nur is a powerful pointer to the failure of Islam to get rid of caste and class divisions in India. Hinduism is blamed for promoting class and divisions in the society and the rise of Islam has always been attributed to the negation of this trait. Nur is highly educated, he possesses a Master's degree. In spite of it he fails to get a job because he is the son of confectioner - a statusless person in Indian society. However, it is a harsh commentary on the hollowness of Indian education that does not fill its beneficiary with any sense of confidence and does not equip him to understand the reality around or encourage him to face the challenges of life. The story also seems to strengthen the traditional view of breed and upbringing as the ingredients of success and progress in great contrast with the modernistic view of opportunity being subservient to talent sharpened by education.

Ananta of *The Big Heart* points to the conservative nature of the north-west Indian society. People who live in constant fear of alien invasions have no inclination to indulge experiments in progression except whatever ensures their physical and material safety. They do not dare adopt reforms in attitude and styles. Moderation and reforms find greater welcome in societies that are not under eternal pressure and threats. In situations and times of threats it is wise to sink differences and individual interest for the integrity and safety of the community. Its dangers soon manifest, however, if the arrangement is prolonged and suppression gets institutionalised—a trait of feudalism. In due course it encourages indulgences which lead to the decay of the system and of the vested interests. This leads to reformist movements by the younger set who has grown up in the absence of the threat perception. This explains a number of social reform movements like the Arya Samaj.

# 'Untouchable'

*Untouchable* (1935) is the first novel of Anand. It was written while he was studying Philosophy in England. He was encouraged to write it by Irene, his girl friend with the promise of marriage. Later, the novel was thoroughly revised on Mahatma Gandhi's advice. The manuscript was rejected by 18 publishers for the sole reason that it depicted the life of a sweeper, a mere mention of whose name would be a taboo in the civilized society of those times. No decent person would read it therefore. Ultimately it was taken up for publication on the recommendation of a friend of India and that of Anand, the famous English novelist E.M. Forster.

The protagonist of the novel, Bakha has been taken from the real life. Anand knew a meek sweeper boy of that name and was affected by his plight. The impression created by Bakha on the heart and mind of young Anand was so deep that he has become an important member of the Anand troupe. He figures in *Confessions of a Lover* and *The Bubble,* the two novels written in autobiographical mode. In *Untouchable,* Bakha is shown to have arrived at an understanding with the elder son of the regimental clerk that he would teach him elementary reading-writing in exchange for a fee of two pice. This clerk's son is no other than Mulkraj whose father was a clerk in the Regimental office. On the strength of the same reason it is possible to surmise that the injured son of the clerk in Untouchable is Mulkraj's younger brother for bringing whom Mulkraj's mother abused and cursed Bakha for polluting him. Similarly the poet, Iqbal Nath Sarshar, who talks of the new latrine-cleaning machine is no other than the real poet Muhammad Iqbal with his rational outlook and concern for the suffering.

*Untouchable* depicts the plight of those suffering under the quadrangular yoke of Indian society. It is an account of a day in the life of a sweeper boy Bakha. Quite early in the winter morning he goes to clean the latrines although he feels like lying crumpled with his English clothes and military boots on, under the torn blanket. But the shouts of sepoys and abuses of his father Lakha compel him to leave the comforts of the bed in the shivering cold of the cantonment town of Bulandshahar. However, he does his job very efficiently and cleanly and there is a general approval of his work. Havildar Charat Ram offers to give him a hockey stick in recognition of his talent and devotion to work. By the time he comes back home he is tired and feels like having some tea. His sister Sohoni goes to fetch water from the upper castes' well. There is already a big queue of untouchable women waiting at the well in the hope of some kind hearted high caste men drawing water from the well and pouring into their empty pitchers. Quite a few pass by but no one has the inclination or the time to listen to their entreaties. Ultimately the priest comes and draws a bucketful and pours it into the pitcher of Sohoni, out of turn, because she is young and meek. The priest also asks her to go and clean his house. Lakha asks him to go sweep the roads and collect the left-over food from the houses of the upper caste men. While on way back home sweeping the roads is done by Lakha and it is Bakha's first chance to do so. He buys a packet of cigarettes from a stall. The fellow overcharges and sprinkles water over the money Bakha puts down on the edge of his stall. He also feels like eating jalebies and buys some. This fellow also cheats him while weighing. He does not know that on the road he is expected to shout caution about his presence. A merchant in white runs into him and makes a scene and slaps him after realizing that he has been polluted by the touch of a sweeper. A Muslim tongawala, however, disperses the crowd by his arrival and cautions him about his obligation to shout his presence. He also feels surprised when another Muslim shopkeeper asks him to light his cigarette direct from the chilm of his hookah.

On his way back he begs for food at the houses he cleans. He receives much curses and abuses. A housewife throws chapatis from the first floor which fall near where her child had just defecated. Another shouts abuses at him for defiling her house by sleeping at her doorstep. At home his father too curses and abuses him for not bringing anything delicious. Disgusted, he goes out without eating because he is unable to forget the scene of the chapati falling near the child's excretia. He meets his friends Chhota, the cobbler's son and Ram Charan, the washerman's son. Though outcastes both, Chhota and Ram Charan are superior to Bakha in hierarchy. But they do not observe this distinction and accept him as their leader. Ram Charan offers him sugar plum which he has stolen from his house where there are celebrations on the marriage of his sister. But Bakha is sad and drifts to Havildar Charat Ram. The Havildar asks him to fetch him burning coal for the chilm of his hookah. He also asks him to bring tea from the cook. He pours tea in a plate for Bakha and asks him to drink it. All this is unbelievable to Bakha who has never been allowed to enter any uppercaste house, not to speak of the kitchen and touching utensils. Charat Ram gives him the promised hockey and he goes to play in the regimental team. There is a quarrel and the boys start pelting stones in which the son of the clerk is injured. Bakha lifts the child in his hands and takes him to the latter's home. But the wife of the clerk starts cursing him for polluting her son by touch.

Sad at the treatment he receives at home and at the clerk's he goes to hide his hockey in the reeds along the marsh.

There, a Christian missionary Col. Hutchinson spots him and brings him to his home with the hope of converting him. But all that the missionary says in praise of Christ seems contradictory even to his small mind. The moment the padre's wife sees him, she shouts abuses and Bakha runs away. Drifting aimlessly, he reaches Gol Maidan where has gathered a huge crowd to listen to Mahatma Gandhi's speech. He is surprised to realise that nobody minds his touch here. A poet talks of latrine cleaning machine. Gandhi talks of the Brahmins cleaning latrines at his ashram. Much of what he hears there convinces him that he will remain what he is but with the latrine cleaning machine he may not have to carry human excretia on his head and may, thus, become touchable.

In the *Untouchable* Bakha has been created as a class in himself, the parallel of which is difficult to find outside the fiction of Anand. He is a scavenger, the lowest of the lowely. He is meek and submissive and not ill-mannered or arrogant. Contrary to his background he is intelligent and efficient as is evidenced in his job of cleaning the latrines. He loves to wear English clothes and wants to be educated. This is appreciable but not alarmingly superb because he is young and lives in a town and his aspirations are generated by his environment. He sees contradictions everywhere and contradictions are the best means of educating the self. At home there is his father Lakha who is abject in his supplications and greedy in his desires. He feels grateful to the upper caste people for the crumbs and torn clothes they throw to the untouchables. His younger brother Rakha is a traditional sweeper boy with his nose running, hair matted and full of lice. His sister Sohoni is graceful in her limb. His friends Chhota and Ram Charan look to him for a lead. Among these people he stands alone, distinguished with a charm of his own. He is liked by the tommies for his clean looks and clean job of the filth he removes. Havildar Charat Singh loves him and sends him to his kitchen and accepts from his hands the chilm and the tea.

Nobody minds his touch at the Gol Maidan where people throng to listen to the Mahatma. The sons of the clerk don't mind playing hockey with him. He is the only species who values education and offers to pay the clerk's son for the lesson the latter would give him. These are healthy influences upon him which help bear with the merchant who slaps him for polluting him by his touch. The priest tries to molest his sister and accuses him of polluting the temple by his presence. The housewife finds it unbearable that he should doze at her doorstep but finds it okay that he should gratefully lift the chapati from where her child had relieved himself. The clerk's wife curses him for rushing her bleeding son home. He does not react except to show his awareness of these tensions. He feels anguished at the hypocrisy of the priest who would accept his sister for sex but finds the whole temple defiled by the mere climbing of the steps by Bakha. He also refuses to accept humbug from Col. Hutchinson in the name of Christ. Even at the Gol Maidan, he does not accept everything that is told except what appeals to his reason and what is directly relevant to his situation.

Bakha, thus, is at once a yogi—a self-restrained, self-knowing and self-disciplined person. He wants to negate the stigma of his being and he is open to all suggestions and possibilities without being in a hurry or excitement. He is not faced with an identity crisis as critics like Premila Paul have tried to make out (17). It would be more appropriate to say that Bakha is Gandhi's ideal hero without knowing it rather than "a Gandhi disciple" as S.C. Harrex calls him.

It is not a coincident that Gandhi comes to address the gathering at dusk. All the incidents take place in the clear day light—the time when the whole social world is awake. The day is the time to tackle problems and find solutions to them. Since the problems of Bakha are not attended to by any of the social pundits and the tomfoolery of conversion being no answer to the practical problems of individuals in a society, Gandhi's appearance as a political leader signifies the evening of social chaos disappearing into the darkness of night with the promise of a new morning of political awakening poised to take over.

# 'Coolie'

*Coolie* is the story of a fourteen year old fatherless hillboy Munoo. He is brought to the plains by his greedy uncle to serve in the household of Babu Nathoo Ram a clerk in the same bank. Since he does not know the ways of towns in the plains and does not know how to behave in educated persons' households, he feels bewildered and blunders at every step including relieving himself by the kitchen door. He lets fall the tea things when the babu's English boss visits as a guest there. He bites the grown up daughter of the Babu while playing monkey and gets beaten for it and outside by the servants from other households as well. He runs away and seeks refuge with Prabha, a childless hill-man, owner of a pickle-factory. He adopts him and dotes on him and Munoo feels relieved of anxieties and uncertainties. But the presence of Prabha's partner Ganpat makes him apprehensive. Ganpat quarrels and misappropriates the capital and leaves Prabha a ruined man. Ganpat deserts Prabha after accusing him: I am through with such scum as you. You are not my class. You belong to the street, and there you shall go. I spit on you. (126) With the closure of the factory Munoo is again on the street and tries to be a coolie in the grain market. He is, however, ousted in the competition for lifting heavy sacks of grain for a pittance. For a little while he plays many tricks to earn a living by lifting vegetable loads, until he meets a circus mahaout who takes him to Bombay.

Bombay proves a nightmare to him with no place to sleep even on the pavement. He finds it 'a land of cruel constrasts, where the hybrid pomp of the rich mingled with the smell of sizzling grease in a black frying-pans' (270); He drifts to a cotton mill in company with another coolie with a family and is employed for his strong and healthy physique. Here he finds that right from the gatekeeper to the foreman and the manager every one exploits the coolies. Blood-sucker pathans and shopkeepers spread their tentacles outside to wring the last drop of blood from the emaciated bodies of the wretches. Those like Ratan who resist their exploitation are dismissed from jobs. There is a strike which is soon turned into communal riot and Munoo too does not escape being hurt. However, an English woman Mrs. Mainwaring takes pity on him lying half dead in the middle of the road. She takes him to Simla and looks after him and makes him her rickshaw-puller. There he is incited to become a communist by an England educated coolie Mohan. But Munoo refuses to take up arms. The strain of pulling the carriage up the steep slopes of Simla makes Munoo sick and he contracts T.B. and dies of it in spite of the cares of Mrs. Mainwaring.

The significant fact about Munoo is that he comes down the hills onto the planes and rolls on to the sea-shore, i.e., Bombay and again climbs the heights of Simla. Both the journeys are, however, performed on crutches—he is dragged down by no other than his own uncle Daya Ram to be tossed and kicked about by all and sundry. This is in sharp contrast with the English woman Mrs. Mainwaring who pushes him up the heights—an act of great courage on the part of a stranger who should have nothing to do with scum and filth collecting on the edge of the sea. She is no missionary and her private life of physical pleasures has no room for coolies like Munoo. Like Bakha, Munoo too does not act or react to various situations and whatever happens to him is accepted only by the way. He does not contribute to the progress of the story. Rather, he is pushed along the course of events like a piece of wood that floats and tosses with the thrust of every ripple and wave. If he finds the edge, it is not his due but only by the way. Thus Munoo is a spec on the large troupe of Anand's world, important to the extent of being not important at all: a coolie here or a coolie there does not make any difference because there are ten available if there is need for one. Munoo's existence in the grain market and even in the vegetable market and the railway station is threatened by competition which he can't with stand. On the pavements of Bombay and on the gates of mills, again he finds himself pushed out as an independent individual. If he agrees to deface himself, as is required of him in the household of Mrs. Nathoo Ram or in company with another coolie who had gone to bring his family, he may survive as hundreds of game-animals in the jungle exist, in proportion to a handful of beasts of prey. Their lot cannot be improved by Prabhas or Ratans or Mohans. Prabha is too weak to safeguard his own interests from his unscrupulous partner Ganpat. Ratan is as worldly unwise as he is strong in limb and morale. He is like a proverbial bull who can umph and sway his pointed horns in the face of an enemy that knows how to overpower and butcher and feast on the fat animal. Mohan is that species who prides in being mental slave to everything, idea or suggestion that comes from the West. His fascination with the West is so intense that he is not prepared even to consider the vast differences in the clime and temperament of the European and the Indian besides the tradition and culture and the lore that shapes up the basic psyche and the personality of the native. But, with his basic native instinct intact, Munoo takes no time to realise that however these people, representing diverse destructive currents, may be amenable to him, he will have none of them as his masters.

Munoo comes as a great question mark on the canvas of Indian life. Like Bakha, he too does not react violently to any injustice or cruelty except when it comes to asserting his manhood among the equals or like when he fights the servant boys at the public tap outside baboo Nathoo Ram's house. Like Bakha again Munoo is highly ethical in his attitude.

# 'Two Leaves and a Bud'

In *Two Leaves and a Bud*, we meet a dispossessed aged peasant Gangu being lured to the tea-estates of Assam, "three days' and three nights, journey from Hoshiarpur." (6). He has a son Buddhu and a daughter Leila besides his wife Sajni. The promise of good wages and huge savings and a free gift of a piece of fertile land are temptations too strong to resist for Gangu. He has lost all his property and ancestral land to the moneylenders at his village and is forced to go to a distant unknown land with a vow that never shall he borrow on interest in his life again. But soon after arriving at Robertson Tea Estates, Gangu starts realising that he has been cheated by the vile Sardar Buta. A coolie, Narain, from Bikaner discloses that once a coolie comes there he would neither be able to go back of his own free will nor allowed to escape. "Nobody's mother or sister is safe in this place."

No sooner than Gangu arrives there, he starts realising that out of frying pan he has landed himself into the fire itself. The wages for working from morning till evening are three annas for Gangu, two annas for Sajani and Leila each and half of the anna for the son! In exchange for this they are abused and beaten and their wives and daughters sexually exploited. The merchants charge exorbitant prices and high interest on loans. Gangu witnesses that a Tibetan's "sack of grain valued at the rate of three rupees a maund comes to six rupees. The whole length of cotton, is worth eight rupees, at 4½ annas a yard. I will give you the whole length because I trust you, but I will put down the price of three-fourths of the length to your debt in my account book, with the interest on the unpaid money at the usual rate of a rupee." (59) Gangu finds that the total income of his whole family does not suffice to buy even the food items. After his return from the weekly market Gangu falls sick and soon thereafter his wife contracts cholera and dies of it. Gangu does not have money to perform the last rites on her body and goes to borrow from Croft Cook, the Burra Saheb. On the promise of paying commission to the peon Hamir Singh and babu Shashi Bhushan, he is allowed to see the saheb. But he is driven out as a disease carrier. He goes to Buta for help and is advised, in turn, to seek a loan of twenty rupees from the bania. Thus, the coolies have no chance of receiving any help from their masters except the abuses and kicks. The voluptuousness and tyranny of the Assistant Plantation Manager Reggie Hunt increase unchecked. Coolie women have to leave their sucklings in the grass, dust and road and cannot even offer their breasts to their babies during the working time. Those who are beautiful and young are either hoodwinked or forcibly taken away as was done to Neogi's wife. They are rewarded trinkets like ear or nose rings and their husbands given land. Those who resent, are hounded, beaten and fined enmass on the point of guns. Their protests invite the wrath of the Sahebs. In the event of less or no work, they are not allowed to leave. Railways don't sell them tickets and authorities and the police always push them back on to plantations. Night vigils are kept lest one escape in the darkness of the night. No assemblies are allowed in leisure time. The government is an active partner in such exploitation and inhuman treatment. A mere attempt of the coolies to protest the ugly behaviour of Reggie is branded 'mutiny' and to control the defenceless servile coolies, the government sends bomber planes and military to contain this 'mutiny'. The governor visits and remits their fines and, grants them bakhshish to win over the coolies with a show of generosity.

De-la Havre is humiliated for showing sympathy with and advocating the cause of coolies. He is dismissed from service and his beloved Barbara, the daughter of Croft Crook, becomes cold towards him. But Reggie Hunt is allowed to indulge all sort of cruelties, bullying the coolies and raping their women. No woman is safe once he casts his eyes on her. He spots Leila in the tea-garden and asks her to come to his house. When she does not respond and runs away to her billet she is chased by him. When Gangu comes in his way, Reggie shoots him dead. The predominantly British jury and the judge, however, acquit Reggie as not guilty of the crime of murder.

The title of Anand's third novel is loaded with significance. For, *Two Leaves and a Bud* (1937) put together is three. Life in this novel is seen from the third angle. The triumvirate of the king, the priest and the man of wealth monopolize the stranglehold over human race. The lord's authority is sanctified by the priest. He, in turn, holds his sway over the ethereal soul of the masses. The man of wealth spreads his tentacles over the material self itself. The three connive, cooperate and complement one another in turns. Gangu, the dispossessed peasant is the victim of feudal and commercial combine. Earlier, Bakha was the victim of priestly religion and Munoo that of the capitalist system. In *Two Leaves and a Bud* it is not only the simple commercialism to the fore, but exploitation on gunpoint.

Gangu is already resigned to his fate, although he has faint hope of a fresh beginning. He is separated from the land that bore him and fed him. Like an enterprising American, he decides to seek his fortune in too distant a place. But, he is too old and like an aged American, discarded as useless impediment in the ways of the youth, he dies a miserable death. Though he does not know even vaguely the reason of his death, it reminds of the Whitman's adventures into others' lands with no sense of sanctity for native life or law against his rapacity and greed for possession of man, woman and material wealth. In this novel as in *Untouchable,* the oppressed class woman is not a taboo for the upper class man. Leila, Gangu's daughter is a tempting game for Reggie Hunt although Gangu himself is thrown out as a carrier of epidemic when he goes to seek a loan for the funeral of his wife and later punished for being a mutineer. Like the Coolie, *The Two Leaves and a Bud* too offers a study in contrasts. Among the Englishmen Croft Cook is interested in gathering as much as he can squeeze out of the poor coolies. Reggie hunt, being not married, thinks only of coolie women to satisfy his lust, even though in exchange for paltry sums or objects. De la Havre, also unmarried, on the other hand, however, is a kind hearted Englishman. He genuinely feels for the oppressed workers and sides with them against his own countrymen and their interests. The real shock, however, comes not from what the alien does to the native but how the native allies with the alien to feather his own nest by baiting his countryman for the alien. The real culprits are, therefore, not Croft Crooks and Reggie Hunts but the Butas and the worst are the Neogis. The latter bully others on the strength of prostituting their wives to the sahibs.

# 'The Village'

*The Village* (1973) is the first of the three books known as the Village Trilogy. It depicts the graduation of Lal Singh as a boy in a remote village Nandpur in Manabad district of undivided Panjab. The people are strong built and hefty and even old men like Lal Singh's father Nihal Singh can carry sacks of grain on their backs for miles. But their lives are marked by woe and misery brought about by merciless exploitation by the rich landlords and other cronies of the British Government. Nihal Singh's fortune is declining through debts and mortgages and the seizures of land by the landlord. Sardar Bahadur Harbans Singh is locked in a legal fight with the landlord.

Lal Singh is the youngest son of Nihal Singh. He is well built and works hard. He goes to the school and has the courage to rationalise issues and face injustice. While working in a ditch hard in the hot sun, he realises the disadvantages of long hair and turban for a peasant. He also does not approve of the necessity of Kara, kangha besides kesa in the changed context. The danger of Mughal assaults and atrocities that haunted Hindus in the times of Aurangzeb, does not exist now. At the first opportunity, therefore, when he goes to the fair in company with his friends, he gets his hair cut. He also buys food off a mussalman's shop when hungry and eats it in spite of being reminded by a Hindu merchant. When he reaches home, however, he received abuses and humiliations at the hands of his parents and brothers. The landlord's son

Hardit Singh blackens his face and the priest Arjan Singh lifts him on to a donkey. He heaves and wriggles and runs away.

During his years of growth, he witnesses how cunningly Seth Chaman Lal cheats the peasants by obtaining their finger-prints on blank paper and bargaining hard for the interest and security. The landlord, on the other hand, is all set to usurp the lands of other peasants and harrass to subdue them by cooking up false cases against them. He, therefore, decides to leave his village when the landlord wants to get him arrested on a false charge of theft of fodder because he had seen Lalu playing with his daughter Maya.

Disgusted, he walks out to Manabad where he meets a drummer announcing open recruitment to British Indian Army. He is a fine, well-built young man 'gem of a man, a diamond, a ruby among men' in the words of Havildar Lehna Singh (198). He is easily recruited for his knowledge of English and mention of his being a Boy Scout appointed by the Deputy Commissioner Mr. Hercules Long. He is further saved by the British Captain Owen from being arrested on warrant for theft. However, he finds the Indian junior officers like Lance Naik Lok Nath in the army to be tyrannical and mean towards Indian sepoys but meak and servile to the British and their government. Persons like Harbans Singh offer good example of it. On a message that his father is seriously ill, he is allowed to visit home. He finds that his eldest brother had been sentenced to die for murdering the landlord's son after catching him and Mahant red-handed in a compromising position with his wife Kesari. His elder brother Dayal Singh's marriage does not take place too, for the mischief played by the landlord's family. His father is delirious on the death-bed by the time his leave is over. He is affectionately seen off at the station by his friends Gughi, Ghulan and Churanji. Within a few days of his return to duty, his platoon is ordered to Europe. Before he leaves, however, he receives news of the death of his father.

*The Village* is a very important novel with rich and minute descriptions of the life lived in remote countryside. The legendary exploitation of the peasant by the landlord and the priest is vividly portrayed in action. Rotting in the slush of remoteness, unconcerned with the benefits of education as an instrument of liberation from taboos, omens and abject servility, the hardworking and honest peasantry is seen being mercilessly exploited and humiliated. No giant efforts are needed to lift them from this mire — A little education enables Lal Singh to see through the cunningness and trickery of the moneylender, the jealousy of the landlord and the lechery of the priest. With his elementary school background, he can talk to the British Deputy Commissioner and the Army officers. The exploiters are scared of his presence as a thorn in the free ways of rapacity, hence wary of his presence.

In *The Village* Anand's ambitions and avenues of hope get more clearly defined. He clinches the issue by openly declaring "the future of the village belongs to these youngmen. I see here, and not, I hope that you will not be angry if I say so, to the greybeards." (p. 161). It is only the youth that can be put on the right path and not the old people confirmed in their distorted views and faulty habits acquired over ages. He also subtly indicates another area that needs to be attended to: the change of attitude from contempt of the fellow Indian to trust and regard in his capability as a compatriot. Indians lack this quality and it alone allows the alien to get the better of them by playing up dissensions and complexes.

Deputy Commissioner Long does not approve of the vain-glorious ways in which the landlord Rai Bahadur Harbans Singh showers his praises and pledges his servility. Captain Owen saves Lal Singh from being arrested even though Captain Puri had already handed him over to the police. It is as much praise worthy of the English character to see through and hold in contempt the Indian meanness as the

English deftness to perceive a situation in which the native emotionally becomes a bonded slave to his patron without whose protection either his own men would roast him alive or the law will seize him from the throat. Thus what Owen does therein lies the secret of British policy, by means of which alone they could rule over this country for so long: by encouraging their Indian lackeys to perpetrate cruelties and injustice on the masses and by protecting the refugee only if he volunteered to die for them.

## 'Across the Black Waters'

After seeing Lalu off in *The Village* on his voyage to Europe, we meet him disembarking in Marseilles, France, along with paternally affectionate Havildar Lachman Singh, God fearing aged Daddy Dhanno, white-haired but clownish Uncle Kirpu Ram and Subedar Major Arbel Singh's son Subah besides others in *Across The Black Waters*. They are warmly greeted by French men and women as the much needed saviours. Before they are transported on board cattle-box trains to the war front at Lillers, they get time to visit the town. Sexually suppressed, strong-limbed youngmen as they are, they prefer to visit a brothel to enjoy white-rose French girls. But, here too, they are cheated by an Indian Dewan, who dupes them of their money. Amidst the white aliens their taboos break as they drink by mouth from the same bottle of brandy from which a French had drunk. They are despatched to the trenches, however, soon after they alight from the trains. Here the trenches are full of slush from rain. The climate is cold too. But they are not issued good, warm clothes, again because Indians incharge of supplies indulge in malpractices and favouritism. They receive much kind treatment from their British officers and local French civilians. Worse are the Indians Lok Nath and Subah who let go no chance to bully and demean their own fellows. There are attacks by and on the Germans. Indians acquit themselves very well earning praises of their officers. There is, towards the end, an attempt at pamphleteering and propaganda by the Germans to create disaffection towards the British among the Indians, particularly Muslims in the name of religion. In the first attack by Indian troops Kharku and Dhanoo are killed. Later Hanumant Singh is shot dead by the Subedar for refusing to fight for unjust British government. The Subedar himself is killed, however, in the offensive immediately thereafter. Lalu also witnesses the suicide by Uncle Kirpu. Havaldar Lachman Singh too dies in action. The narrative ends with the arrest of Lalu as a wounded war-prisoner in a fierce attack on the Germans.

The chief concern of the novel is to illustrate how the simple, ignorant peasant folk get indoctrinated into believing that they, as the loyal soldiers of the mighty British King, have no need to know their destiny, no need to bother about their conscience and no need to find out the cause for which they have instinctively committed to sacrifice their lives. But, the British officers' proverbial sense of fairness on the personal level, towards the subordinate and his concern for the soldier's welfare is all that makes the difference in winning him over the loyalty of the native in the face of the petty squabbles and mean conduct of Indian officers towards their brethren. In this novel, Anand seems to raise a vital issue--why the Indian is more than ready to leave his home, his village and even his country; and feels more happy working for and laying down his life for others with hardly any remorse! He answers this anxiety by giving away the impression through the text that it is because the Indian distrusts and fears his own people, Lalu finds his own story repeated in Dhanoo's case more than the alien, who lost his roots with his eviction from his tenancy and thus drifted to become a labourer. He then enlisted as a sepoy to die unknown and unsung in a foreign land. Subsequently, he witnesses the murder of Hanumant Singh for betraying the pricks of his conscience from which he had begun to suffer. The suicide of old Kirpu after he is humiliated by a mean petty officer Lok Nath to cover up the lecherous intentions of his Jamadar Subah, is also a shock to him.

Though no harsh criticism of the conduct of Indians is offered here, their treachery borne out of their meanness towards their compatriots, has been amply demonstrated: the poor, afflicted and ignorant peasant is lured to enlist on false prospects of land grants and exaggerated remuneration and other facilities. After he is enlisted he is constantly persecuted in an atmosphere where he finds himself between the devilish demands in the name of army discipline and the lynching society which he cannot go back to. Thus, a situation has been created in which "ordered about by the Sarkar, they were as ready to thrust their bayonets into the bellies of the Germans as they had disembowled the frontier tribesmen, (*their own countrymen*) for the pound a month which the Sahebs paid them (133).

## 'The Sword and the Sickle'

Anand is satisfied with the portrayal of conditions of embarrassment and the subtle causes leading to it, so far. It becomes his endeavour, however, to visualise as to what could be the results of such an explosive situation. Thus the third and the last part of this Village trilogy *The Sword and the Sickle* assumes great importance. After his release as a prisoner-of-war after the victory of the British, Lalu arrives in India with great hopes of honours and land-grants for his services. Soon after his arrival, however, he realises that the sarkar has been playing hoaxes on the innocent poor Indians. After being in Europe in different situations, his perception of the reality has sharpened. His demobilization on a small pension but with no land-grant and that too on the intervention of Babu Khushi Ram on his behalf, leaves no doubt about the vile nature of the British government, in his mind. Away from home and its persecutions while in Europe, he realises the futility of suffering meakly in an already rotten atmosphere. His mother dies. His surviving brother Dayal Singh turns an ascetic. And Kesari, with her parents, realises the need to become a revolutionary. His uncle Harnam Singh has already formed a rebel club. Maya is a widow now, but still full of love for him. His friends Gughi, Santokh, Jitu are all revolutionaries now. On the assurance of a job for his maintenance by one Prof. Verma, a communist ideologue, he decides to leave Nandpur for Rajgarh where he would be in the employ of Count Rampal Singh, an eccentric revolutionary brother of the late ruler of the state.

Maya agrees to elope with him and aunt Ajit Kaur gives him the bridal jewellery for Maya, left by his mother. Lalu and Maya accompanied by Verma reach Rajgarh, where they are received by count Rampal Singh, his attendants and comrades. Rampal Singh has been organizing dispossessed peasants and murderers into revolutionaries. A one-eyed peasant Sukhua has been turned out of his tenancy by the manager of the estate of the Nawab of Nasirabad. Rampal Singh, along with his comrades including Lalu visits the Nawab to persuade him to restore the tenancy to Sukhua but in vain.

Lalu busies himself in creating an awareness among the peasants, of their plight and its causes. Rampal Singh addresses the crowd in the mela gathered to have a bath in the river to wash off the evil effects of the Sun-eclipse. People listen but do not feel provoked to assault the sadhus. The mother and the younger brother of the Count do not approve of the conduct of Rampal Singh. Since he is anti-establishment, the government too does not like it and pressurises his younger brother, the caretraker of the State, to oust him from the Palace. Lalu preoccupies himself with work among the peasants and remains mostly away from home, leaving Maya to herself. They have been lodged in an isolated corner of the palace. One day the police comes to arrest Lalu for abducting Maya on the information collected from his revolutionary friend Gughi and uncle Harnam Singh under arrest now. But the Count's successful hoodwinking of the police-inspector who had got employment on the Count's elder brother's recommendation, saves the situation. Meanwhile, Sukhua's son is beaten dead by the manager of the Nawab. Lalu and Rampal Singh plan to take the dead in procession to Prayag as a means of creating an awakening among the peasants. A Congress lawyer Srijut Ladli Prasad Tiwari agrees to arrange a reception for this march at Allahabad. But the men of the Nawab disturb and it becomes a misadventure with the shooting to death of Nandu by the manager. The corpses are abandoned in the Ganges but the party cannot return to Rajgarh because they see the police waiting and calling them on the banks. They decide to drift aboard a country barge to Prayag. Rampal Singh had planned to receive them in Allahabad. When they reach Rajgarh House, there they learn of Mahatma Gandhi's programme of dining with the untouchables at Anand Bhavan. The Count brings about a meeting of Lalu with Mahatma. Lalu and the peasants are invited by Gandhi to join the feast. But the great man sees no point in visiting the troubled areas. In stead Jawaharlal Nehru agrees to visit the suffering ryots. The police with the help of feudal forces manages to puncture the tyres of the car and Nehru cuts short his programme and goes back to Allahabad without inaugurating the Kisan Sabha.

Lalu's involvement with revolutionary activities keeps him away from Maya. She has already been spotted by Kunwar Birpal Singh, the younger brother of the Count, and seduced. To remove the obstacle in the way of his free enjoyment, he gets Lalu arrested for assaulting the Co-operative Bank peon. Birpal Singh rapes Maya while Lalu is in jail. They are however, released by the English magistrate due to the influence wielded by the Count, much to the chagrin of feudal forces. The chaos increases with the morale of the comrades of the Count boosted so much that Sukhua beats Birpal Singh in his palace. They also feel emboldened to travel without ticket. Much of the success of these revolutionaries is due to the immunity the Count enjoys. In a sweep, however, the government in collusion with Birpal dispossesses Rampal of his property. Rampal is, thus, set on a mission to regain his property by wielding influence on governmental quarters. Things have changed, however, and he is arrested along with other peasants. Lalu too rushes to Rae Bareilly where he has weird encounters with the police at every step. Peasants in huge numbers throng the town and demonstrate before the jail for the release of their leaders. Lalu too is arrested ultimately and in jail he hears of the birth of his son to Maya.

In this novel Anand tries to lay the blame for most of the ills and weaknesses of the poor peasants at the door of religion. This novel depicts the revolution and revolutionaries in their true colours too. Revolution in this country, as all the other leads are, is centred round the traditionally rich and influential.

The chief protagonist Lalu, however, is the standard bearer of the novelist. It is against the above background, therefore, that we have to view Lal Singh's conduct. He alone is a genuine revolutionary who had learnt much earlier to rise above the self. His own comforts and possessions mean nothing to him. He does not behave hysterically even after learning of the rape committed by Birpal Singh on his wife Maya. After he learns of the arrest of Rampal at Rae Bareilly, he rushes to reach there in spite of the desirability of meeting his wife before leaving. It opens up the whole question of the honour of the woman vis-a-vis man. A wife is not entitled to the protection of the husband if the younger brother assaults her or betrays his intentions towards her. A brother, even though a criminal, gets precedence over the better half. Rampal makes no pretence to learning and lays no claim to heritage. He speaks a language which is easily understood by the masses. His actions and conduct endear him to whoever he moves with. This indicates the populist nature of the leadership which is not necessarily enlightened.

Rampal Singh is surrounded by the most degenerate and vile cheats whose only interest is to enjoy the food, wine and company of a rich man who has allowed them to hang on to him. Rampal too cannot be said to be a revolutionary since a revolutionary is a man of genuine action volunteering to sacrifice the self for the emancipation of others and for a larger cause of humanity. Rampal know nothing of the history, tactics and requirements of revolution. He is not well read.

For him the revolution means trading filthy abuses and wining and dining with a few good-for-nothing peasants and flatterers around him that too only so long as he has his riches to himself. At the first shock of dispossession he rushes to seek restoration of his privileges from the same British government against whose stability he professes to work and exert.

The novel succeeds most in portraying the abject poverty and exploitation of tenants and small peasants of U.P. Their plight worsens with their failure to rise with encouragement and support. All this is due to their merciless suppression by the feudal forces and disintegration borne of meanness and cunning dictated by their need for self-preservation.

The novel also exposes the fake leaders like Ladli Prasad and to some extent Nehru who desert the scene at the first encounter with trouble. It also derides scholar revolutionaries like Verma whose whole concept and action is confined round the table within the forewalls of their study.

# 'The Big Heart'

*The Big Heart* is the story of Ananta, a coppersmith and his community-men's backward ways. They live in and around Kucha Billimaran in Amritsar. Some of the coppersmiths have travelled outside. But most of them have come back after losing everything or have become Babus and Sahibs. Some of the young boys go to factories and lead a life of comfort and fashion. Among these is Ananta who has returned from Bombay with a widow Janaki. He has taken Janaki for a wife and is criticised by the elder members and young men of his community. The influence of the workmen's city of Bombay is evident upon him. Most of the other youngmen too are faced with the problem of work. This situation has arisen because of the opening of a factory by Gokul Chand, the Kasera and Murli Dhar, the coopersmith. With the installation of machinery, the work that used to be available to the self-employed coopersmiths, is no longer available to them and they are faced with the problem of subsistence. In addition to the loss of work opportunities the wages too have been lowered at a time when cost of living is increasing. Since most of the work is done at the factory, more and more coppersmiths are getting out of business, leading to conditions of penury. This causes bitterness among them. The younger generation is more vocal and, together they blame the opening of the factory and the policies of Gokul Chand and Murli Dhar. They consider the factory and its owners their enemies.

The general resentment against the factory and its owners

increases also because only the close relatives of the owners get employment in the factory in the face of ever growing number of job seeking thathiars. This situation compels moderate trade unionist Ananta to organise the community into a union so that a solution could be negotiated with the factory owners. The efforts of Ananta are appreciated by the employers, particularly Khushal Chand and Hans Raj and poet Puran Singh Bhagat. Their opinion and advice is generally acceptable to most of the sensible members of the thathiar brotherhood. But a few hot tempered and block-headed persons like Ralia and Viroo among the thathiars and, communist leaders like student Satyapal and professor Mejid feel perturbed over Ananta's influence. While the ignorant condemn him for keeping a young virtuous widow who is unapproachable to them, the hot-headed communists dismiss Ananta's approach for a negotiated settlement as chicken-hearted and a sell-out to the capitalists. If Ananta succeeds in persuading the unemployed into forming a union, the communists would lose an excellent opportunity to create anarchy and destruction through the block-headed coppersmiths in the name of Revolution. Both Satyapal and Mejid, therefore, vehemently denounce the ways of Ananta, whose patent refrain is 'to have a big heart', so that they may have the coppersmith youth in their communistic fold. They succeed in inciting Ralia, Viroo, Mehnga and others to wreck the machinery in the factory. Ralia does it under the influence of liquor and temporary insanity. When Ananta intervenes, Ralia smashes his head on a machine until blood gushes out of Ananta's skull.

*The Big Heart* assumes importance for several reasons. It is the only novel in which Anand openly denounces the student-provocateur brand of communism. In fact, he sacrifices a precious life to establish his preference for peaceful methods of settlement of issues over the bloody means advocated by street-communists lured by cheap popularity and instant action. He leaves no doubt about the undesirability of the destructive and violent ways to seek solution to the intricate socio-economic problems. The backwardness of the coppersmiths is not due to lower wages and lesser work alone which phenomenon is of recent origin. Their backwardness is also due to a lack of trust in and respect for the fellow coppersmiths. Murli Dhar considers it below his dignity to invite the members of his brotherhood at the betrothal ceremony of his grandson. He cringes and begs before the slightly upper caste kasera Gokul Chand to grace the occasion by their presence for which he decides to dissociate himself from his dirty brotherhood. Among the piece-workers also Ralia and Viroo consider it their bounden duty to oppose every proposal that comes from Ananta who is one like them but has better perception. The primary reason for this opposition is Ananta's keeping of the widow Janaki who is available to them as a common property since she exclusively belongs to Ananta. He is also hated because he has been in Bombay and has better understanding, wider experience, lots of guts and a very big heart. He could be considered a jewel in the crown, if his community were a little educated and enlightened. The backward communities are, therefore, themselves to blame for their miserable plight and lower place in the social hierarchy. Ralias and Viroos are, in fact, instruments of self-destruction since their urge to destroy the machine is more powerful than the pleadings of saner elements around them. Anand quite unambiguously states that the machine has to be enslaved for the greater good of the greater number rather than to be submitted to or destroyed. Its destruction would not increase the social wealth although a few more individuals may get temporary succour after such a happening. Moreover, it is not the machine that deprives the worker of his wages but the greedy and cunning owner of it that plays foul. However, he too succeeds in duping the worker because of the distrust of the worker on a fellow worker and his preference to capitulate before the owner.

Ananta is a singular type of hero whose murder is unintentional. Maqbool Butt too dies in the *Death of a Hero.* But Maqbool's is a voluntary sacrifice and his murder is coolly intentional. Coolie Munoo also dies but his death is due to consumption which could be the result of several factors. The death of Noor, the "hero" of *Lament on the Death of a Master of Arts* is also due to consumption. His death is reminiscent of the death of Munoo the coolie. The death of Munoo appears, however, more dignified than of Noor. Munoo braves many hazards of employment even though uneducated and an orphan hill-boy. Noor is highly educated and has many relatives on his side including his parents, wife, grandmother and parents-in-law. No other hero of Anand dies. In *The Big Heart* the narrative covers the happenings in the life of Ananta in one day, that, incidentally turns out to be his last day. During the course of this last day of his life the finer characteristics of Ananta's get revealed: like his large heartedness, wider understanding and immense patience. In *Untouchable* too, the narrative accounts for a day in the life of Bakha. But that one day might not be much different from any other day in his life. However, that day proves much significant in his life. Bakha, moreover, is denied the facility of assertion and influence which is available to Ananta in abundance. Thus Ananta is a unique creation--an embodiment and an ideological incarnation of Anand's socio-philosophical being. *The Big Heart* is also significant because it is an open assertion of the faith in Gandhian philosophy as a panacea in the filthy marshland of isms. The futility of Marxism and the undesirability of unbridled capitalism have been brought to fore at a great cost—at the cost of a noble, simple, clear-headed man that could lead the larger humanity on the right path. But it is not allowed to happen by the very forces which cry themselves hoarse as the champions of humanism.

## 'Seven Summers'

The story of *Seven Summers* (1951) is told by its central character Krishna. Assuming an autobiographical tone, he tells the story of his childhood with the assurance that he has retained the memory of all that happened to him and around from the age of five years. Krishna's father is the Head Clerk of 38th Dogra Regiment. He belongs to a rich family of Coppersmiths a four storied house in Kucha Fakir Khana at Amritsar. His father was born of the blessings of a Muslim Fakir and was married while still at school. He is the only literate person among the illiterate soldiers of the Regiment. He is, thus, very important to them because he writes letters and lends money to them. He being the Head Clerk can also recommend the cases of promotions and favours for any body. Krishna's mother Sundari is the eldest daughter of Nihal Singh a noble Sikh landholder of Daska village near Gujranwalla town. She is an orthodox woman and worships the images of Ram, Krishna, Buddha Chist, Guru Nanak. Krishna's eldest brother studying medicine and is already married to an illiterate girl Draupadi, the daughter of Babu Bhagat Ram. On the biddings of his wife Harish abandons studies and his father gets him appointed Assistant Jailor at Lahore on an honourable pay of thirty five rupees a month while his own pay is eighteen rupees. Krishna's elder brother is Ganesh, who is easily dominated by him because every body pampers Krishna. He had a younger brother Prithvi who died in infancy. However, his mother had already had a big belly by the time of Prathvi's death and soon Shiva was born.

Krishna is a beloved child not only of his parents but of the neighbours and other relatives too. He is loved by Gurdevi, the childless wife of another clerk Chhattar Singh who is interested in back biting and usurping the Head Clerk's post. His aunt Devaki too has no issue and loves Krishna. His uncle Pratap Singh, however, is a drunkard and non-vegetarian food is cooked in their house in contrast with Krishna's house where only chapatis and lentils are cooked with occasional vegetables and fruitsweets gifted by various subordinates and other favour seekers. By virtue of his position, Krishna's father wields a lot of influence and always keeps close to British Sahebs because he wants to prosper in wealth and increase the prestige of the family. Cloth for the family comes from the Regimental storekeeper's bounty and is sewn by the regimental tailor. Ramzan at the threat of holding up the payment of his bills; shoes for children from some stray cobbler against the help in getting him permission to sit in some corner.

Krishna is called Bully by his father and all those who love him. He gradually grows into a real bully. One day he is beckoned by Ali, the Regimental saxophone player's brother, to eat the earth and then the thorny cactus fruit. When the thorns pierce his lips and tongue he starts crying and betrays Ali. On the biddings of Ganesh he lets the kitten fall in the well and tells mother who has to donate a gold cat in penance. At the "Sparrow show", he is not frightened by the growls of tigers. At the school, on the first day, he impresses his teacher by reciting the poem which no one else could, but he is beaten by Ali and others outside for slapping them on the orders of the teacher. The Sahebs love him and always shower favours and privileges upon him, like giving a ride on his horse by Owen, or in his gig. The other boys feel scared of him because he betrays them like he did when the Pathan kept him bound for stealing maize stalks in company of Ganesh and Ali or when he spoiled their games of war with bows and arrows by going with stick for a sword and climbing the 'fort' on the peak to conquer it. Once he was hit by a stone thrown by Ram Charan at Bakha and was injured in the head and remained confined to bed for five months. But he passed his examination by making up at home under the supervision of his father. Thereafter, he goes with his brothers and mother to his grandpa Nihal Singh to enjoy for sometime, particularly after the examinations are over. His uncle Sharam Singh comes to take them to be present at his marriage and also to borrow some money. On reaching Daska, he plays with his cousin Durgi and feels the warmth of her affection. His youngest uncle Sardari Singh sings for him the legendary song of Heer and Ranjha. He also plays with buffalo Suchi and has the experience of riding its back into the pond. He is rescued, however, by his uncle Sharam Singh in time. Krishna also receives love from his second uncle Dayal Singh who grinds almonds to paste and offers him the sherbet. His dislike of the sherbet earns for him the nickname of city bred. Soon, however, there is a quarrel between his mother and widow aunt Amrit Kaur. His mother too is accused of having become a miser and cunning after marrying a city baboo. The insults mount and they decide to leave before the marriage.

Krishan also tells of the privilege of his birth being attended to by an English nurse who went back to England. This fires his imagination and he is encouraged, since his early childhood to go to England. The effect of the stories of the birth of Lord Krishna told him by his mother, of Raja Rasulu's legends and continuous pampering by one and all is that Krishan, the narrator of the story, considers himself born to do some thing special and to be a Messiah to the suffering humanity. With his growth in years he finds that people look at him differently now than they did when he was a childling. He becomes conscious of the wretched nature of his father and the household. He is no longer treated with the earlier love and affection by his father. His tyrannies, on the other hand increase and his meannesses become obvious. The desire in Krishna arises, therefore to be free of this bondage. The opportunity comes early with the declaration of war and the posting of his father to the Frontier further West. The children and the mother are sent to his parental house in Kucha Fakirkhana at Amritsar.

*Seven Summers* is an important source of information about Anand's early childhood. It is an important document recording his growth and various influences that shaped his life, opinion and philosophy of life. It also traces the genealogy of Krishan Chander. The roots of the family tree go back to Daska where old Baba Nihal Singh stays in the Haveli. Nihal Singh has been a crusader for freedom from the ferungees and has always believed in moral uprightness. He is a great supporter of self-respect and hates usurpation of others' properties and subjugation to and flattery of the British, to thrive on the crumbs thrown by them. Harbans Singh, his cousin has illegally taken into his possession most of Nihal Singh's lands because he has the backing of the British. His sons Sharam Singh, Dayal Singh and Sardari Singh are the younger brothers of Krishna's mother Sundari. She has been married to a person who has sold himself out to the British government and wants his children to rise in life following his own example. But these children have more of Sundari's qualities than those of their father. This is evident at the first sight, as Dayal Singh says, "they look more like their mother's than their father's children. (190) Sundari is a rebel "like her father Nihal Singh who" "fought for Khalsa" (190). Because she, like a conscientious wife, does not tolerate castigations on her husband, she is driven out of her parental household, and all the women join in their drive against her. This is symbolic of sentimental victory of nationalistic forces over flatterers of the British, as Krishna's father boasts himself to be.

Krishan is stubborn, dashing and winsome in his demeanour. Even as a child he is conscious of how to draw the maximum advantage out of a situation, even at the cost of his adversary, be it his own brother or dirty Ali. If his charms win the Englishman's heart, then he should build up his fortunes on it. He is successful in pushing out his elder brother Ganesh from everybody's favour and getting the place himself. Only once he fails to dislodge Ganesh from the favours of Durgi. He, therefore, becomes the cause of permanent abandonment of Durgi in the withdrawal of his mother and children from Nihal Singh's household itself. This state of childish pranks soon yields to a maturer state of consciousness of various desirabilities and undesirabilities. After coming back from his grandpa, therefore, Krishna wants to be free from the oppressive atmosphere of his father's house. Understanding of past events of deprivation of children and mother of good food, clothes, shoes and various other items necessary for the enrichment of lives but which have to be paid for, dawns on him. The earlier love for father gradually changes into intense hatred of this man who sacrifices his own happiness and comforts besides becoming indifferent to the happiness of his family members, for the superficial notion of honour and rise in status built up only on the crutches of British patronage.

The *Seven Summers* is a close study of child psychology. It delineates upon the fact that children know their interests well and, left to themselves, are fully capable of looking after themselves. Krishan cries only when some elderly person is around but sucks his foot when hit against the boulder and forgets it because he knows his father will not be moved by his barefootedness. He pounces upon his mother to suck the other teat when he sees one is already in Prithvi's mouth. It is a remarkable book so far as it records the growth of Krishan as a bully. It is also an analysis of various contrasting influences that shape his consciousness and contribute to his grasp of intricate facts like the donation of a gold-cat for a kitten drowned by him or the lost silverspoon being found at the door-step only after his mother conveys her readiness to donate it to the temple. The greatest influence on him comes of his mother's faith in the quality of the gods and prophets of different religions. It is truly remarkable to read of the imagination of Krishan being fired to meet his fairy godmother who has gone to England.

# 'Private Life of an Indian Prince'

*Private Life of an Indian Prince* (1953) is the story of an Indian autocratic ruler of a small hill state Shampur on the borders of Tibet and Kashmir. He is introduced to pleasures of flesh rather early in his life. He name is Ashok Kumar but he is popularly known as Victor or Victory. The British government has conferred on him the rank of Major General. His first wife is ten years older to him. She has no children and is mostly devoted to puja path. His second wife is about his equal in age and has a daughter. Since there is no male issue as Tika or successor to the gaddi, he is married to Indira the daughter of the ruler of a small state in Bengal. A male child is born to Indira, so she is known as Tikyali Rani. However, this male child is allowed to die due to the machinations of Ganga Dasi, the mistress of the Maharaja. She is the daughter of the state priest, seduced very early in her life and has been with many men at many places. She is older than the Maharaja but possesses great charm. She is a clever woman and has ensnared the young Maharaja so much that he refuses to part with her. Ganga Dasi begets a son and a daughter by the Maharaja and is anxious to ensure the recognition of her son as heir apparent to the gaddi. Her hold on Victor is so great that he does not show any happiness and orders no celebration at the birth of his son by the legal Rani but publicly proclaims his illegitimate son by Gangi to be his successor to the throne. On a petition by Tikyali Rani, however, the government of

India refuses to recognise Gangi's son as the legitimate successor to the throne. Ganga Dasi conspires to increase her hold on the Maharaja and humiliate the Rani. Victor who is infatuated to Ganga Dasi starts selling and buying properties in the name of Ganga Dasi besides conferring many other benefits and privileges. But Gangi is too cunning and given to the pleasures of the flesh to be exclusively devoted to one person. She is capable of seducing anybody and offers herself freely to different people including the commander-in-chief Raghbir Singh who is a cousin of the prince; Popat Lal Shah the Diwan, Bool Chand the Political Secretary to the Maharaja and even with Kurt, a one-time visitor besides innumerable others. Victor is so indulgent towards her that he does not mind her sleeping with others if she comes back to him. But Gangi deserts and bullies and befools him as she pleases. Ashok is so much given to the pleasures of sex with her that he indulges seduction, abduction and even rape on any pretty or young woman he spots. He suffers humiliations and lowering of prestige on this account but is helpless and incurable. Ganga Dasi is his passion.

The story opens at a time immediately after the British have left, leaving India and hundreds of feudal states free to assert their sovereignty. Shampur being strategically located, various forces covet to get their stranglehold over it. The Congress government of India with Vallabhbhai Patel as the Home Minister is trying to integrate various princely states with the rest of the country and make India into a unified Republic. The princes have been asked to accede to India and have several privileges like their privy purses and personal properties assured to themselves. But Victor is set to keep his state free and toys with the idea of getting it the status of a buffer state. To achieve his end he orders army manoeuvres and invites Americans to canvass their support. He also lets loose police repression on the restive subjects and arrests leaders of Praja Mandal, puts them to sulk in dark and stinking jails. Interestingly he intersperses his actions and conversations with expressions of sympathy for the poor and support for democratic processes. But he hates communist guerrillas even though he occasionally feels for them too and regrets afterwards that he did not join communist guerillas to preserve the sovereignty of Sham Pur in the face of danger from the Bania raj of Shah, Boolchand, Birlas, Tatas etc. However, his position becomes pathetic and his plight pitiable with the signing of the instrument of accession and the flight of Ganga Dasi with Boolchand. With his sulkings and moanings for Gangi he becomes intolerable and is sent to England. But he manages to avenge the flight of Gangi by getting Boolchand murdered in India. He is called back. But he goes mad and hysterical even while flying and is admitted to the mental asylum in Poona.

*Private Life of an Indian Prince* is totally different from other novels of Anand. The story is narrated by Dr. Hari Shankar, the personal physician and close friend of Maharaja Ashok Kumar who is his confidant and a witness to the most intimate actions on the part of the prince. The story is based on a traumatic experience in the personal life of Anand. He had come to India to settle down and then to call his English wife Kathleen Van Gelder and his daughter. Here he fell in love with a clever hill-woman and went to divorce his wife in England so that he could marry this woman in India. However, by the time he came back, this woman had left for Paris with a French lover. Anand was shocked and had a nervous break down. On the advice of his Greek nurse, he wrote his anguish out in the form of *Private Life of an Indian Prince*, which says Anand, rushed out of in one month. But the novel, as it is, portrays the darker side more of Ashok Kumar than that of Ganga Dasi, the hill-woman. She is an unscrupulous common whore fated to float in the higher circle of the princes and noblemen. Before she had access to the palace of the Maharaja of Shampur, she was used by several herdsmen in the hills until she was sold in marriage to a Brahmin peon Shiv Ram. She ran away with a wrestler and gambler Motilal. After he became bankrupt she lived with Kishan Chand, an accountant in Imperial Bank who in turn shared her with quite a few businessmen and professionals. Then a Lahore Seth film-maker Seth Ranchod Das gave her a part in film. Thereafter she went from one lover to another including a Parsi confectioner Homi Mehta, film writer Inder Nath and the second Rani's brother. In the opinion of Dr. Shankar and Victor, Ganga's life has been miserable and pathetic. He thinks that this woman was at once sadist and masochist....no one noticed that she was a schizoid or split personality." (p. 143) But the important aspect of the whole affair is the male's desire to dominate and order over the female. The slightest attempt to deviate from or resist the male's exclusive ownership of woman becomes a pretext for ballyhoo and the whole social fabric is made to crumble because of the female's conduct. The primary objective of the novelist, therefore is to invite attention to this irrational approach by man towards woman. This is amply demonstrated by showing the eighteen year old Tikyali Rani as the worst sufferer at the hands of her husband for being a devoted wife, an intellectual companion — she is a graduate - ; and for accepting all humiliation and exclusion and deprivation at the hands of a male who sets premium on debauchery, and unbridled sexual orgies. Heavens start falling when his pet ageing whore is not available to him one night. However no ripples are caused when young Indira sulks for months, cast away in some desolate building. Further, the 'Suraj Vansi' descendent of Ram's unscrupulousness in having even a washer woman is not questioned whereas Gangi's passing affairs with other males within the regalia becomes a great crime!

It appears that Anand wants to de-sexualise the sex that overdominates the Indian psyche by over-sexualising his narratives. The hunger of sex is more powerful than the hunger of the belly. The more it is shunned and tabooed, the more it plays havoc with man. More murders and treacheries are committed in the name of sex and most of the history revolves round sex as the generative force than all the ethical and philosophical issues put together. The message which Anand seems to convey after his understanding of the West is to seek freedom from sex by taking it as it is and not by making it a monster.

# 'The Old Woman and the Cow'

*The Old Woman and the Cow* (1960) later published as *Gauri* (1976) is the only novel in which he has exclusively focussed on the plight of the most neglected member of Indian society—uneducated peasant woman of the hills. Hillmen are generally known for their hard life, suppression and docility. Hill woman's plight is worse. She works hard, is beautiful in limb and complexion and yet she is a 'wife to whosoever needed her'. She is, thus, the most helpless and the most exploited person. Gauri is the daughter of a widow Laxmi under the care of a bully Amru. Her father was poisoned by Amru in complicity with her mother for his wealth and the lustful life Laxmi wanted to lead. She is married to Panchi, a parentless small peasant of the neighbouring village Chota Piplan, much to the displeasure of Amru who had designs on her. There is a general belief, supported by the chain of events that follow, that Gauri is an unauspicious girl. After her marriage with Panchi, there are quarrels and asaults among Panchi, his aunt Kesaro and uncle Mola Ram on various pretexts centering round Gauri. So, Gauri and Panchi are ousted from the house. They go to live with a Muslim potter Rafique Chacha, much to the resentment of the whole Hindu community. In her first year with her husband, there is acute drought and Panchi goes broke. At the first mention of her pregnancy, she is turned out by her husband for fear of feeding an additional mouth. Insulted, she seeks refuge with her mother, who under the influence of Amru, agrees to sell her to a rich aged merchant of Hoshiarpur. Much against her wishes and resistance she is bundled out to Hoshiarpur on horseback. By the time she is delivered in Hoshiarpur, she is sick. The widower merchant Seth Jai Ram Das calls for doctor Colonel Keshav Mahindra and tries to rape her thereafter. But she stubbornly resists and succeeds in getting out to the doctor's nursing home. The misfortune dogs her heels there too. For, there the junior doctor Batra sets his eyes on her and one day tries to rape her. There is a big commotion in the whole town and the hospital establishment is broken. Gauri goes to work with colonel Mahindra as a nurse. Meanwhile, there have been much needed showers. Panchi decides to bring back his wife. When he reaches his mother-in-law's place in Pipla Kalan he is given a good beating by Amru's hired bullies. The police appears and Laxmi is directed to restore Gauri back to her rightful husband. Laxmi, accompanied by old Chaudhari Adam Sing goes to Hoshiarpur to recover Gauri. However, when she is restored to her husband, she is derided and her husband is taunted by the whole village for having lost her chastity at so many places she stayed at, in the town. Except pleading her chastity, Gauri cannot prove it. She is constantly harangued in the image of Sita after her return from Ravana's place. Ultimately, Panchi is overcome by the tirade of the villagers and assaults her and turns her out. Gauri decides to go back to Mahindra's hospital rather than suffer humiliations at the hands of ignorant and mean minded villagers.

It is thus a very powerful story. It not only highlights the weak position of woman in Indian society but also the utter helplessness in which she invariably finds herself. Whether devoted as Gauri is, or a whore as her mother is, she is a victim of male brutality. She has no status at all. Even in the matters of the sale of the daughter, her voice or protests have no meaning. In the background of the events, Gauri's unflinching and simple approach to the problem of dignified existence is a very remarkable achievement. Though uneducated, unprivileged and inexperienced in the wicked world of man and life in towns, she is able to wade through the filth with simple clarity of mind and purpose. Thus Gauri redeems the honour of the woman and shows her a nice way out of her predicament--economic independence as the answer to all her miseries, her illtreatment and negation of her status. Its message is both revolutionary and a retort on behalf of the Indian womanhood which is variously projected as *abla* (weakling), Durga (Goddess of fierce strength) and Kali (Goddess of Massacre of evil). Gauri is neither a weakling nor a demon. She accepts suffering in its stride, resists where called for, protests when the occasion demands and submits too. She does not hesitate to turn Kesar-out of her house since the latter's primary aim is to create dissensions and hatred in the household of Panchi and Gauri. She protests against her sale by Amru and offers physical resistance to Seth Jai Ram Das at his house and Dr. Batra at his hospital in measured degrees and effectively prevents them from raping her. The most charming quality, which is generally found in the heroes and heroines of Anand, is Gauri's balanced behaviour and self-composure in the face of calamities. Unlike the traditionally portrayed Indian woman, she does not, overawed by her own sense of helplessness, surrender to the tyrant except her husband to whom she is bound by marriage. Nor does she go to any extremes of either killing the oppressor and exploiter or committing suicide. Iconoclast as Anand is, through Gauri he attains his goal better by simultaneously depicting the goddess's failure in coming to the help and rescue of the devotee after the invocation, in the image of Krishna running barefoot to save the devotee elephant from the clutches of the evile crocodile. Whatever happens is normal and within the limits of credibility. No miracles happen. Thus, it seeks to strengthen the idea that not gods but normal human efforts are required to ride over day to day problems of life in the evil world that we live in.

*Gauri* is also the only work in which we find some traces of the craft of fiction. It has a plot and the action at the later stages takes place along two parallel tracks. The chronology of events until Gauri is made to leave Panchi's place follows normal course. It bisects into what the principal character is going through and what happens in the void created by her exit. When Gauri is restored her household, however, comes the peak of crisis when she is finally turned out and leaves for a known destination with confidence. By closing the narrative at the peak of katharsis, Anand succeeds in keeping the narrative interesting as well as purposeful.

# 'The Road'

*The Road* (1963) is being built to link village Govardhan with Gurgaon, so that milk and other produce could be transported to fetch better price and as a consequence prosperity may come to the whole of Govardhan. But caste prejudice plays havoc here too. The Sarkar is disposed towards improving the lot of the low castes. Its officers, Block Development Officer Diwan Roop Krishan and Engineer Tulsi Ram therefore seek the support of Lambardar Dhooli Singh, a high caste Rajput, to gather workers for building the road. The payment is meagre but the untouchable *chamars* of the village agree to break quarry stone and lay the road because no other work is available to them except to toil on the fields of the high caste on the wages of little grain at the end when the crop is harvested. The building of the road is considered a great loss by the other better caste people because it deprives them of the almost slave labour for their fields as well as a chance to earn wages by working on the road. The landlord Thakur Singh, his son Sajnu together with Lachman, the son of the Lambardar and cowherd Mahesh, Daya Ram, Ram Niwas etc. are agitated over the fact that one of their own castemen Lambardar Dhool Singh has succeeded in winning the favour of the Sarkar and the trust of Chamars of the village. Thakur Singh tries to win over Pandit Suraj Mani to bringback Dhooli Singh to the fold of the caste so that Chamars could be easily cowed down to abandon road building. The alternative to it would be to excommunicate the Lambardar from the brotherhood. But the priest is wily and cunning and a double dealer. He is not prepared to support or condemn any side openly. He is interested in exploiting everybody in the name of religion. The landlord, therefore, incites his son Sajnu who, in turn wins over Lachman, the son of the Lambardar to his side and the two set the huts of *chamars* on fire.

Bhikhu and his mother Laxmi's hut and the goat are burnt too. Like the rest of the untouchables, they too become homeless and miserable. Laxmi is god-fearing and is highly conciliatory towards the high casteman for the fear of losing the next life. But Bhikhu is a little educated and young. He does not believe in God and caste and also does not bother about the traditional high ups like the landlord and the priest. After the huts are burnt the poor helpless harijans gather in front of Dhooli Singh's house, his wife Sapti and daughter Mala have been incited to desert him and have gone to stay in the temple. Dhooli Singh, therefore distributes all the clothes of his wife and daughter among the Harijans and sets up a settlement on his own lands. After hearing the cries of Harijans, reaction sets in the hearts of Sapti, Mala and Lachman and they return to their home. Lachman decides to work with the untouchables, breaking stones. Sajni too goes to join his friend. Both Lachman and Sajnu are betrothed to each other's sister respectively. Dhooli Singh is, by nature, amiable towards every-one. The priest too decided to sail with the wind and goes to Dhooli Singh with the expectation of managos. There he is given not only a basket full of mangos for the temple but is invited to eat some there itself. Soon all the untouchables are invited to join the feast. This fact becomes known to the landlord Thakur Singh and others through children and he falls sick. There is gloom in the house for now the marriage of Sajnu as well as that of Rukmani can not take place with Mala and Lachman respectively. Sajnu deserts stone-breaking because he finds the wages very low. The landlord sees the doom of the mankind. Rukmani can do nothing but weep after Sajnu announces he would not allow the marriage to take place.

In the Epilogue Bhikhu is shown leaving the village permanently for Delhi because nobody there would care for or ask the caste. He is hit by the brass-tumbler full of water offered him by Rukmani but kicked by Sajnu injuring him on the mouth.

# 'Morning Face'

*Morning Face* is the second stage in the childhood of Krishan, the third son of army Head clerk Ram Chand. The story is the extension of the earlier narrative of Seven Summers in which the birth and growth of the baby Krishan were recorded. It had ended at a time Ram Chand's regiment is moved to far away Peshawar and the family left at Amritsar. Ram Chand escorts the family to Amritsar where he has ancestral property and cousin Partap and his wife Devaki, a childless beautiful loving woman. They are welcomed by the coppersmith brotherhood to the fold of Arya Samaj after they renounced their allegiance to the Agha Khan. Both Ganesh, the elder and Krishan are admitted in the fourth standard at Pandit Baij Nath High School run by Pandit Ram Nath, an old class-mate of Ram Chand because Ganesh studied in a remote border school without English as a subject of study. Krishan is smart and aggressive in showing his superiority over Ganesh, and this competitive spirit dominates their relationship at home and outside home. The third, Shiv, is too small to go to school. It is the earnest desire of Ram Chand to see his children well settled in life, holding respectable positions in the government so that the prestige of his family may be enhanced.

Ram Chand is the President of the local Arya Samaj also. Later, after a bomb is thrown at the Viceroy and the name of Arya Samaj is associated with this act, he severes his connections with it. However, Krishan likes the company of *Arya Samajis*, particularly Dev Dutt, for their advocacy of widow re-marriage and abolition of superstitions prevalent among Hindus. Krishan is loved by his aunt Devaki who eats and offers him meat and wants to adopt him. But Ram Chand has his designs. He very cleverly offers Ganesh for adoption with the intention of grabbing Devaki's jewellery and money and property through Ganesh as the legal claimant. All the family jewellery and property had gone to Partap because of Koko Killi, the aunt of Ram Chand, who is still a follower of Agha Khan and a custodian of the property donated in the name of Agha Khan. Krishan finds that his mother is very superstitious and believes in ghosts, seance and priesthood. Devaki, aunt Agi and courtesan Nawab Jan actively participate in invoking the spirit of long dead fakir Sain Lok to visit upon and speak through Aqi. Thereafter, when Kaushalya falls sick with fever after touching the burnt up bones at the cremation ground, the mother forbids Krishan to go near her, believing that the spirit of the dead person had caught hold of the girl. She hangs amulets round children's necks and puts kajal in their eyes to protect them against the evil eye of the people, when the visit of the Inspector of Schools to examine children, is announced. At this visit they are promoted to the next higher class after kicking and failing those who are not properly dressed. At about this time, Krishan's father is transferred to Chitral. Ganesh and Krishan are left with their elder brother Harish. He is an assistant jailor at Ludhiana. Shiv is taken along for being too small.

At Ludhiana, Harish's wife Draupadi develops instant liking for Ganesh for being vegetarian and a dislike for Krishan for the opposite reason. Ganesh is, therefore, invited to eat in the kitchen. But Krishan and Harish are served outside. After marriage Harish had gone to study medicine at Agra. But Draupadi dissuaded him against leaving his studies before completion. She also remains childless. There is no harmony in the relationship of Harish with Draupadi. He goes to visit courtesan Mumtaz. She too is devoted to him. One day

Krishan too manages to follow Harish and his friend Noora to the house of Mumtaz and her sister Moti. There he is played and fed well as a child and develops affection for Mumtaz. This development creates bitterness at home and Draupadi calls her father to take her home. She is not allowed to go back to her parents, however, because they still follow Aga Khan. So, she prevails upon Harish to take her along for a week to the town of her parents where she would stay with the relatives of Harish but visit her relatives during the day. Once she goes, however, she does not return until Ram Chand goes to escort her back on the sad occasion of Partap's death.

Partap is simple hearted, hard working coppersmith. He loves Krishan more after the death of her only child Kaushalya. But he dies one day after drinking the milk offered by Devaki. It is believed that she mixed poison with the milk in conspiracy with her relatives because he was demanding division of ancestral property. Ram Chand suggests that Ganesh will perform the last rites of Partap with the intention of making him legal heir to Devaki's property. After both Krishan and Ganesh go back to Ludhiana, Gainda Mal and Achint Ram propose to marry Ganesh with an orphan girl under their charge. Harish accepts it and is advised by his father to inform Devaki since, she is the foster-mother of Ganesh now and would therefore, incur all the expenses on his marriage. At school in Ludhiana, Krishan finds many teachers with different temperaments, tastes and outlook. There is one master Buddh Singh, a hefty Sikh who is a spy of the police on the nationalist teachers. He beats children mercilessly and demands Christmas gifts and private tuitions in great contrast with another master Shah Nawaz who teaches with love, smile, ease and assurance. Once, when he beats Krishan and the monitor Batalia and others mercilessly, the matter is reported to the Head Master who suspends Budh Singh. But Budh Singh becomes bold and invites children at home to practice homosexuality.

At home Draupadi leads a frustrated life because Harish not only does not love her but also because he loves Mumtaz. She slaps Krishan for speaking well of Mumtaz and he falls sick. He is shifted to Noora's house where he is nursed by Mumtaz but, when there is no improvement in his condition, he is taken to Amritsar where Ganesh and Krishan's initiation ceremony is due. Because of the orthodoxy of the mother Krishan's head is shaved and he is bathed with cold water for the initiation and sacred thread ceremony. His condition becomes worse and hopeless and he is taken down on earth. He is, then, shifted to Jhelum Cantonment hospital where he is put under the special care of a Christian nurse much after the attempts of his mother to try a priest, a Muslim peer, an earthen lamp on the cross-roads, charity of clothes and even a goat's sacrifice fail to bring about an improvement in his condition.

He is now admitted to the government High School here. At Jhelum, his father coaches him hard for matric examinations. Krishan earns praise of Raja Fazal Mohammad because of his dress and proficiency in English. Here also he finds some of the teachers loyal to the British and some nationalists. His father's position is in doldrums at this because British encourage differences and disaffection between Garhwali and Dogra soldiers. Ram Chand favours Garhwalis and is afraid of Dogras' attempts to raise and encourage his rival Chhatar Singh. There is disobedience by Garhwalis and they are killed in hundreds. British and Dogra officers are arrested but Ram Chand escapes court martial on the testimony of the British Officer. Harish too is betrayed by Draupadi for selling cotton bales worth 20000 rupees belonging to the jail. But timely intervention of the British adjutant on behalf of Harish due to the approaches of Ram Chand saves the situation. Ram Chand further secures a job for Harish in the Army.

The tense atmosphere at home is relaxed and mother feels like going to Hardwar. Ganesh is sent to Harish and Krishan to Devaki at Kanowan where she is getting a well dug for the Mahant of Nandgir. Krishan realises that it is all enjoyment at Kanowan with the Mahant drinking hemp and almond paste and Devaki and Ananta living like husband and wife. He rides the horse of the Mahant there and finds he has secreted in his clothes. Both Ananta and Devaki tell him of his graduation to becoming a man. Ananta offers him whisky to drink. The water is struck in the well after going much deeper. It involves an exorbitant expenditure of more than ten thousand rupees. His experiences here create in him an urge to write poetry and a novel around Devaki and Ananta with Mahanta as a villain.

Back at Jhelum, he meets Bakha, the simple-hearted sweeper boy devoted to him. He is the captain of the hockey team but is the easiest target at any quarrel in game or otherwise. Krishan likes him and agrees to teach him. Thereafter, Krishan develops a boil on his head and is treated by young Dr. Chuni Lal and lovingly cared for by his wife Shakuntala. Chuni Lal and Shakuntala are thorough nationalists and Arya Samajists. Krishan feels encouraged in his anti-British sentiments in their company at home and also in company with Lala Kedar Nath at school. He becomes interested in the meaning of Philosophy as a quest for the meaning of life. A procession to protest against the Rowlette Act by Lala Lajpat Rai passes by the school. Krishan and his friends Inder and Mughees jump the school wall to join it. They are caught by the police and rusticated by the Head Master. They are taken only after Captain O'Sullivan, Ram Chand's officer recommends. The latter is half English and half-Irish and is sympathetic to the cause of India.

Ganesh's marriage takes place in the atmosphere of disturbance and tension with the result Ram Chand and

Harish have to rush back from the marriage party in the middle. Their leaves are cancelled because of demonstrations against Rowlette Act. Krishan too is apprehended and caned seven times for staying out in curfew. Dyer is given the charge and the Jallianwala Bagh massacre takes place. Ram Chand also feels disturbed and shaky in his loyalty to the government because of the ever present danger of court martial. But things calm down and he is awarded Distinguished Service Medal and recommended promotion from Havildar to Jemadar. The Regiment has returned from Egypt and because of the shortage of housing Ram Chand is shifted to the quarter in the followers' line. There Krishan becomes a friend of Bakha and other low caste playmates with whom the whole family feels at ease. But his father is worried about Krishan's increasing indulgence with nationalists. After the examinations are over, therefore, he is sent to Kangra with Babu Khushi Ram. However, he gets fever there and is taken back by Ram Chand. He finds that Dr. Chuni Lal and Shakuntala are leaving after being sacked by the government for their nationalist views and pride. Kedar Nath also leaves. Ram Chand, however, desires his children to rise to the opportunity and try to become Assistant Extra Commissioner, a judge or something like that. Krishan, however, rejects to be what his father desires. He wants to go to England. He wants to write poetry and be a free soul.

*Morning Face* is a narrative of the events in the life of Krishan subsequent to *Seven Summers*. The trend of dotage towards him continues in this book also with minor exceptions of a few people's indifference or slight disliking for him. His father, Harish's wife Draupadi and their like do not exude warmth towards him except the minimum affection that is claimed by any child at that age. This is a sign of the growth of Krishan, not only in physique but also in perception and worldly wisdom. The only thing that distinguishes him from his class is his claim on love of every woman in spite of the fact that he is not deprived of his mother's which may create a longing for someone else's love. His brilliance in the class room is apt to invite the wrath of some of his class mates. The important clue to the study of Krishan, however, lies with Ganesh. Krishan is presented largely in relation to Ganesh—his dullness, elderliness and stereotypedness as compared to Krishan's brilliance and ebulliance. Krishan's growth—both physical and mental—and the alertness of his faculties is however, abnormal. At matriculation he starts longing for woman's flesh and secretes while riding the horse. Even so, the ease with which every woman rushes to hold him in embrace and to open herself can only be considered an excessive indulgence on the part of mature Indian woman starving of such experiences. Besides, there is overlapping and spill over of various incidents and episodes from *Seven Summers*. Devaki's relations with Ananta are open and nobody bothers himself much about them. As in the preceding novel, Krishan falls seriously sick on the nick of the annual examinations, and is sent out during the holidays only to come back unexpectedly early. Chatar Singh's plottings against Ram Chand manifest with horrible consequences in this novel. Ram Chand, however, emerges highly successful out of these and other dangers, due to his great capacity to move not only his inferiors but mostly his superior officers. There was not much scope for concentrating upon the various aspects of the education and the system prevalent when Krishan was quite small. In the morning face, teachers and superstition are the main targets of attack. The teachers are divided not only on communal lines but also in their loyalties to the nation and to the British government. An attempt has been made to expose the policy of the government to pamper Sikhs against Hindus and Muslims and Muslims against Sikhs and Hindus. Master Budh Singh, a Sikh teacher, enjoys full immunity against sodomising and beating children shamelessly because he is a spy of the government. Against this an excellent man Head

Master Abdul Hamid is punished with a transfer for taking cognizance of the mistreatment and demand of gifts by Budh Singh.

The farce, (*the pakhand*), of feasting well-fed Sadhus, priests and peers and seeking their intervention to fight diseases; sacrificing goats and giving clothes in charity for recovery of health from serious sickness; blackening of eyes and tying of amulet as a protection against evil influence, invite the author's criticism and exposure in this novella. It appears that the author is laying a cornerstone of social reform in this novel which he calls the first in a series of seven novels to be known Seven Ages of Man. By means of Krishan's recurring sicknesses and the almost uniform reaction and recourse to superstition by his mother and other women and total ineffectiveness of these tantrums, he attempts to drive the point home that indulgence in such practices means not only offering oneself for exploitation but also inviting the disaster quicker than if it were treated scientifically.

Morning face is also in the form of chronology of events in the history of the family of Ram Chand. But, the narrative follows a little complex pattern by switching over from one scene of action to another because of the dispersal of important characters at different places. The overall impression sought to be conveyed, however, remains unimpaired. By weaving and linking the interaction, Anand has been able to maintain the essential unity of action that terminates with the book itself and is not repeated or followed automatically in the next as appears inevitable in the overall pattern.

# 'Death of a Hero'

*Death of a Hero* is set in 1948. There has been an attack by Pakistani armed raiders on Kashmir. The border town of Baramulla has already been captured by them with the help of fifth columnist Ahmed Shah, former activist of the National Conference, a political party of Kashmir and, Sardar Muhammad Jilani, a rich man. These Pakistani Muslim invaders loot whatever they can lay their hands on and kill whoever resists or does not follow them. They abduct and assault Hindu Brahmin women besides looting and killing innumerable Muslims. This strange conduct of Muslim brothers from the neighbouring State of Pakistan raises doubts in the mind of a young political activist Maqbool Sherwani. In the wake of the attack, he too runs away to Srinagar like most others, but returns to his home town immediately after meeting his leaders of the National Conference. His decision to return is an act of great courage and sacrifice because he knows the Pakistanis would he in occupation of his town. On his way to Baramulla, he reaches a small town of Pattan and meets a couple of shocked left-over persons. He meets the cookshop owner Mahmdoo, his son Gula and the pro-Pakistani teacher Ishaq. He rouses them to organise for resistance and decides to go to Baramulla, at a great risk to his life. On the outskirts of Baramulla, he sends Mahmood and Gula to the town while, he himself hides in the fields for fear of identification and discovery. Early in the morning, however, he reaches a smoke-billowing Christian convent. Except a couple of servants like Salaaman Rehti, all the others have been killed. He borrows Rehti's ladies bicycle and rides it in the direction of his house. He crosses the river and finds Syed Muratib Ali's carpet-factory has been burnt down rendering several poor workers jobless. He has a talk with Muratib who is prepared to help the cause of Kashmir with money because he is weak otherwise. Among other friends the lawyer Ahmed Shah has already joined Pakistanis and Ghulam Jilani has no courage to go against his father. Maqbool rides the bicycle further and is intercepted by Pakistani Pathan soldiers at a tea-shop. By the time they discover his identity, however, he is out of their reach and inside Jilani's house. Here he finds Ahmed Shah and Khurshid Anwer waiting for Ghulam's father to bring the extortion money. With the help of Ghulam he is saved in the name of the guest and helped to smuggle out under a *burqa* (shroud) and escorted in a tonga by Ibil, an old servant and his wife Habiba. No sooner does he reach his home, however, he is surrounded by Pakistanis. He runs away through the roof-top but slips in the slush of an open gutter and caught and locked in a dingy dark stable-prison. Ahmed Shah tries to convert him to Pakistani side in the name of religion but he refuses. In the middle of the night, he is shot dead just before the advance of the Indian Army. No opportunism is involved in this thinking. It is a matter of conviction, the logic of which is unambiguous and as easily perceivable as not to be missed even by his enemy Khurshid Anwar and Ahmed Shah. They find it difficult to counter the argument of Maqbool that,' I put Kashmir above everything. I have principles.'(52)

These are no mere words but a testament of conviction for which Maqbool is ready to lay down his life. His return to his hometown at a time when it is in the grip of enemy testifies to his courage to rise above the self with full knowledge of the peril. To the last minute Maqbool does not budge an inch from his stand and refuses to join the Pakistanis even though he has no firm idea of a way out of the present situation. He has no concrete information of the possible arrival of Indian Army that could motivate him to act. In stead, he is mentally prepared to die. In fact he is more interested in being killed than to suffer humiliation at the hands of Kashmiri turn-coats and Pakistani invaders. He has no doubt that his end has come after his capture. The thought of prolonging his life by agreeing to be a betrayer does not occur to him and much before he knows the manner in which he would be tried and executed, he writes in his diary, "My little sister, Noor, we shall not see each other."(78)

This act of martyrdom is a manifestation of a rare quality of Maqbool Sherwani that puts him above all the other heroes of Anand. No other hero of Anand displays this clarity of vision and understanding of the value of principles in the life of a man. He is neither a passive sufferer nor a theoretician. So long as he is free, he does his best to preserve his freedom. Cowardice does not come near him after he loses his freedom. His fierceness in upholding the cause of his motherland at the cost of his life is exemplary and opportunists like Ahmed Shah are secretly scared of him. He is, therefore, done away with unwarned in the darkness of the night just before the arrival of Indian Army.

# 'Lament on the Death of a Master of Arts'

*Lament on the Death of a Master of Arts* is an account of the last few hours in the life of Nur, the son of a confectioner—the Chaudhari of the shop-keepers. He is educated by his father for the degree of a Master of Arts, with the primary aim of securing a respectable. government job like that of a Deputy Collector. His father is a tyrant and a miser who keeps humiliating him for not being able to secure any job. Nur's mother died when he was a child and he is brought up by his grandmother. His father never sends presents of sweets to Nur's teachers or hire their services for private tuitions. His clothes too are old and unimpressive. He was, therefore, always punished by his teachers and not much favoured by others. His father, the Chaudhari is so self-centred as to marry Nur for dowry, even though the latter is unemployed. His wife Iqbal is gentle and submissive and as much a victim of her parents' treachery who marry her with the hope that Nur would secure a government job. A daughter, Rashida is born to them in due course although Nur remains jobless.

The primary reason of Nur not securing any job is his pedigree. He is the son of a confectioner who has no status in society. Government jobs are given to those who wear good clothes, who belong to good white collar families and those who can secure letters of recommendations or on the intervention of influential persons. Academic qualifications and excellence have no weight against the aforementioned qualifications. Ultimately, with much cringing on the part of his father and father-in-law he is appointed a clerk in the post office. The shock of this realization makes Nur sick and he develops the dreaded disease of the lungs. Day and night he thinks about his rejection, inferior place in society and his helplessness. Added to it is the cruel attitude of his father who keeps abusing him and humiliating him for providing a worthless son. This attitude of the society kills within him the desire to live and Nur prays for death. He doesn't want to live to be condemned by everyone. He laments the fact of his birth in his poem "Why did you drag me into the dust by making me an M.A... ."

We meet Nur when he is bed-ridden and streaks of blood with the cough come out. His childhood friend Gama visits him. He had left the school after persistent failures at the fifth standard and ran away from home. He too realises the present education being of no use. At the last hour Dr. Pachkanwala comes to examine him. The doctor knows and even confides to Nur's father that his last moments have come but not before he has claimed his fee. Soon thereafter, Nur, already weak and emaciated, dies and the women start beating their breasts — a performance which they had come prepared to do even while Nur was alive.

The duration of this long short-story is hardly a few hours. The hero, Nur comes from the category of Dostoevsky's sick heroes and his reactions and convulsions follow the pattern of *Notes From Underground*. He is dying not only of physical consumption but is sick to the depth of his soul. His complaint against society, the government and God is identical and his statements are not only sweeping but betray his sick mentality. While he deserves the maximum sympathy even without his complaint, he does nothing to win or to illustrate. Since he is on his death-bed, very little is expected of him.

However, somehow, his fast journey to death lacks the element of conviction since it happens to a young meritorious man who has just entered the portals of life. He has a young devoted wife and a daughter to live for although he has no mother and would not like related to a narrow minded father. It would be a dangerous conclusion to draw that the young generation of a nation does neither have the guts and the talent to fight their way to attain something for the society through the self. It is a sad commentary on the plight of the teeming millions who do not get any opportunity to display and use their talent in the service of the society that supports them. Thus, the novel portrays the failure not of Nur but of the system that throws up weaklings who can not withstand scrutiny either of the system or that of the Nature.

Nur is the victim of the suppression of his uneducated father in spite of the support of all the other members of the household like his grandmother, wife and friends like Gama. Gama is strong in body as well as in reason. He is more practical in his approach. Nur, however, does not feel enthused to live even after Gama stays with him for so long. He is overcome with a longing to die. A vital question is thrown up by this novel in the form of 'why the evil triumphs over the combined goodness. Why Nur is inclined to be depressed rather than be enthused when he ought to opt for the latter course!' This will to assert, to affirm by the essential goodness is conspicuous by its absence in *Lament on the Death of a Master of Arts* more than in any other novel of Anand. Even an untouchable Rakha's blood boils with rage when he is slapped by the merchant on the road and indications are that he would have surely retaliated had the man not disappeared so swiftly. But Nur's outbursts take the form of his own laments on his life and a complete loss of a desire to revive his interest in life. Added to this weakness is the absence of drama in this novel wherein lies the strength of Anand's art. The novel fails to evoke the desired impression, therefore, not only because it is set in an unrealistic situation but also because of unmerited haste on the part of the novelist to rush through the idea without allowing it to develop into its full lengths.

# 'Confession of a Lover'

*Confession of a Lover* (1976) is the story of a young boy, Krishan Chander Azad who goes to seek admission in Khalsa College, Amritsar. His father, Ram Chand is an Army Officer and wants his second son to become an ICS officer in the service of the British Government of India. He belongs to the backward community of coppersmiths but has risen remarkably with a Meritorious Service Medal in recognition of his loyalty to the government. He is educating his eldest son Ganesh to be a doctor from Agra Medical College. But Krishan is very buoyant and self-conscious. He has suffered the punishment of seven strips in connection with the Jallianwala Bagh incident. He has already met Gandhi and claims to be the greatman's follower in non-violence and in the freedom movement. His father is a Hindu but his mother comes from a Sikh Jat family. Earlier they were the followers of the Muslim leader Agha Khan, but they have come back to the Hindu fold after great penance and, dread any association in any form with the Muslims, lest it be interpreted as their intention to be closer to the Muslims.

Young Krishan, however, is not inhibited by these taboos and meets, eats and sleeps at the Muslim places. On the first day in the college, he suffers ragging at the hands of old boys. Noor Mohammad, the son of a Muslim confectioner too is a sufferer but he feels impressed of the courage and presence of mind of Krishan and becomes his admirer and friend. In the College, Principal Walters and Professors Henry, Teja Singh,

Bhatia like him. But a few teachers and students, mostly obscurantist Muslims and wealthy men's wards, jeer at and manhandle him whenever an opportunity presents. In the College and even at the other meeting places, Muslims, Sikhs and Hindus are divided into groups vociferously supporting or opposing Gandhi. But Krishan always scores over his detractors with the help of spontaneous support he can attract and also because the atmosphere is surcharged with nationalism. Gandhi is a rallying force. Principal Walters and Prof. Henry have great reverence for Indian culture and philosophy. They support Indian aspirations for Independence. Though the College is chiefly financed by the feudal Sikhs, most of the College staff and students have progressive views. The Principal invites Mrs. Annie Besant, an English lady who later becomes a leading figure of India's struggle for Freedom, to address the students. Though she scrupulously avoids saying anything against the government, she exhorts Indians to wake up to their former glory. However, Prof. Teja Singh feels so much inspired that he declares his fight against corruption at the Chief Khalsa Diwan by joining a reformist organisation Shiromani Gurudwara Prabandhak Committee. This declaration creates a storm. The governing body of the College suspends Principal Walters, Profs. Henry, Teja Singh and also Bawa Harkishan Singh for defending Walters at the governing body meeting. The students under the leadership of Krishan go on a strike and a satyagraha until a compromise is reached. All the teachers are re-instated. However, Walters and Henry are sent back to their parent department and Lalla Jag Mohan is the new Principal. The hawks make an issue of it to Krishan and his friends for letting down the strikers. Since most of them talk of violence, Krishan withdraws his participation.

In Amritsar Krishan stays with his aunt Devaki. She is a young childless widow. She loves Krishan for various reasons. Her property and youth attract the whole of the thathiar brotherhood including Krishan's father. She is constantly chided and tortured on various pretexts like visits of a bad character Ananta and Nargis, the young step-mother of Noor. She too goes to Noor's house and sleeps there once, when Krishan lay there down with fever. She has been made to accept Ganesh as her adopted son and spend on his marriage as well as on maintenance. As penance for the sin of visits to and by Muslims, she is forced to spend huge amounts on feasting Brahmins and lighting the sacred fire. The brotherhood chief wants to be her guardian—'They all want to be her guardians!' (Krishan) however sees through this game and objects by shouting, 'She is a widow!' and 'innocent!' 'Does not know the way of the world!' 'We will look after her... and take our little commission. . . . ' Humiliated, she commits suicide. Since Krishan and Noor are close friends, Krishan has no restrictions in Noor's house. He meets, chuckles with and eats at the hands of the females of the house. There he meets Yasmin, the younger sister of Nasim, the wife of Noor. He falls in love with Yasmin although she is betrothed to a Railway Guard Gul Mohammad of Lahore. Both develop strong feelings for each other and she comes to see Krishan at the house of poet each other and she comes to see Krishan at the house of poet Iqbal in Lahore. The poet expresses his desire for their marriage. Their love intensifies so much that Yasmin is invited by Nasim to Amritsar at Nasim's place and all of them go to the ashram of Beas Guru, the spiritual guru of Krishan's uncle Dayal Singh, at Beas. There the two enjoy love-making to their heart's content. The husband of Yasmin, however, suspects infidelity on the part of his new wife. Next time they plan to meet in Kashmir. Nasim goes to escort her from Lahore and finds her murdered. Krishan and Noor come back and find both their respective communities tense and the police on Krishan's trail. The brotherhood castigates him and his father slaps him and also his mother. He feels hurt. He has already passed his B.A.

with First Division. He rushes out of his house, loiters and reflects. He decides to go and study the problems of life and death and their meaning in the free atmosphere of the West. He visits Iqbal who encourages him with a hundred and one rupees for pocket expenses and promises to send maintenance for one month. Principal Jag Mohan too encourages him with three hundred rupees and an overcoat. His mother gives all her savings of five hundred and pledges her earrings for more. At the station all his friends, teachers and even his antagonists come to bid farewell to him.

*Confession of a Lover* thus, becomes an important document of the graduation and confirmation of a rebel. It can be aptly called a portrait of a rebel as an adolescent. It has been written in a truly confessional mode and has autobiographical overtones. Unlike other novels, it is divided into twelve chapters. Though these chapters follow a chronological order, their contents do not follow that pattern. Adopting the camera-eye technique, Anand focusses and juxtaposes situations and personalities in contrast. Life is seen in formal and informal social contexts as well as at the emotional level. Krishan's personality develops without inviting any constraints. The approach is simplistic and impositions have been avoided. The cosy atmosphere of the family has been enhanced by retaining familiar names and relationships. Even habits and temperaments are the same. Thus, the surviving ascetic brother of Lalu from the Village Trilogy, Dayal Singh appears in his usual role. Krishan's mother is one of the three daughters of Nihal Singh. Her brother and Dayal Singh are natural uncles to her progeny. Bakha, Munoo, Prabha and his pickle factory too are there to ensure the familiar setting.

The issues and concerns brought to surface are, however, unusual and defy anticipation. For Hindu-Muslim tensions, following and opposition of Gandhian means of freedom are not as important as the youngmen's defiance and ignoring their elders in the matters vital to individual as well as social well-being. Krishan's sensuousness notwithstanding, his intense love for a Muslim girl even after knowing of her betrothal and subsequent marriage, birth of a child and miscarriages have a deeper significance. Together with it, his involvement in matters of philosophy, journalism, love and poetry, physical fights and satyagraha as a young college student project his image as a healthy-minded and pure-hearted youth capable of tackling problems of life at any level. He has high opinion of himself but he does not betray much egoism except what is warranted by his urges. As a student of philosophy and logic, he does not show his unconcern for physical needs. He does not create a utopia or take refuge in one. He is swift and does not mind drifting in his quest. His quest, however, is not of the surface but a fundamental one: seeking to know the how and why of Life, Death, Happiness, Sadness—all those issues that have attracted the greatest sages of India and yet remain unsolved. Krishan, however, begins with two advantages over the great Indian philosophers: He begins with God discounted and goes in his quest not to the Tapovan in some dense forest or to the heights of Himalyas but beyond the High Seas into an alien civilization. This position had not been taken by anyone in India: although the intents have been the same: to attain objectivity. The virtues of synthesis had all along been considered taboos hence abhorred as unholy. Thus, Anand moves one step ahead in the direction of unknotting the centuries-old stalemate by working the Western plough to break the hardened layers of Eastern soil.

## 'The Bubble'

After reaching England, Krishan notices many differences between the pattern of life at home and abroad. *The Bubble* (1984) is an account of his stay in England. He is introduced to Prof. Dicks, the professor of philosophy, by Prof. Faver, the economist. He notices the behaviour and conduct of his countrymen who try to imitate Englishmen in their dress, greetings and food-habits. Most think of sex and debauchery since it is considered no taboo there. He himself has sex with Evelyn, the daughter of his landlady. His friend Nikhil introduces him to famous critic Bonamy Dobree. He is admitted to the course and scholarship is recommended to him. He also decides to shift to Mrs. Lowe's lodgings. After some-time Dicks sends him to stay with Reverend Thomas. This first part of the narrative named 'The Exile' (Letters to Noor) is told in the form of Diary and is named 'The Ascent of Mount Snowdon, (Krishan's North Wales Diary). He receives warm welcome from Thomases. Reverend Thomas is quite busy with his religious preachings and propagation. But Mrs. Thomas is very affectionate and even defends the Hindu faith. Here too he meets an Anglo-Indian scholar-teacher Lucy Gray who has been in Madras. She is emotional in her attachment to Krishan but has the natural weakness of a cross-breed to have too high an opinion of her-being white and Catholic. On an expedition to the countryside with Lucy on his motorcycle, he meets with an accident, and finds Lucy's first concern is to attend to his wounds. Thomases too pray individually for his recovery. He realises that Hindus in his country would have gathered to see tamasha with no one coming forward to help the wounded, under similar circumstances. He develops feelings for Lucy but finds that she loves Robert Peel, a gay. Here he meets Irene Rhyes, the step-daughter of Prof. Richard Rhys, the Evolutionist.

Part Three: 'Babes in the Wood' is in the form of narrative by a third person omniscient writer. Irene is too free with sex and instantly establishes relationship with Krishan. In *Confession of a Lover*, he had started writing a novel The Absent one. After falling in love with Irene, he starts writing his novel around himself and Irene. She has artistic bent of mind and a free soul. She encourages him to write his novel—'oh, you must write about him...About them all. They seem fascinating. I will type the book for you... And if you can get it published, I will marry you..'(152) Irene is jealous of her mother and ever since she met Krishan she moves with him although she permits anyone to have sex with her. Krishan's wealthy friend Mehta too has sex with her besides Solomon who had it at Watz. On the political front, there are attempts by patriotic Indians like Krishan and Mehta to mobilize public opinion to propagate the cause of India and counter attempts by the stooges of India Office to sabotage such attempts.

Part Four: 'Thieves of Fire' (Diary of Journey to Paris and Back) opens with the arrival of Krishan and Irene in Paris. This part is again in the form of impressions recorded in the diary. Krishan meets here American novelist Gertrude Stein. He also meets young French poets Tristan Tzara, Andre Breton and Aragon. Here Krishan has a weird experience: he is enticed by a prostitute but much against his wishes his organ fails to wake up. He walks out only to find his pocket is picked. They leave Paris after learning of the death of Irene's father.

Part Five: 'Conversations in Bloomsbury' opens in

London. The death of Prof. Rhys is a great blow to Irene and she leaves Krishan and goes to Anglessay. Left to himself, he meets a communist girl Eltie Helman who is selflessly devoted to her job of selling communist literature and would not leave her work for a few minutes. He meets E.M. Forster who wishes to read his novel. Krishan meets Virginia Woolf and J. Krishnamurty too and finds Wools's advice preferable over Krishnamurty's. He also attends a meeting organized by Krishna Menon and addressed by Bertrand Russell to form the India League. Russell's wife Collette is very affectionate towards Krishan and exhorts him to go see Irene in Ireland. Thus the scene shifts to Dublin and the next part is called 'Dublin Diary' (Playboy of the Western World and Dierdre). Like any other Irish national, Irene too is interested in her country's freedom. This is another strong reason she loves Krishan as a man from a wonderful land under the unjust occupation by the British. But her tramp ways attract the police, she is arrested and charged for smuggling arms. Here, Krishan meets W.B.Yeats, the poet of Irish aspirations, who finds Indians dignified. He also has intimate and prolonged meetings with Gregory the playwright, Francis Stuart, Lian O'Flaherty, George Russell, novelists and T.S. Eliot the poet. After moving and conversing with them his concepts get clarified and self-confidence enhanced. In spite of the best efforts of lawyers, Irene is sentenced to ten years in jail and he returns to London. His love for Irene is so tense that the next part is dedicated to Irene: 'Journal to Irene.'

Away in London and with no hopes of meeting Irene, Krishan indulges introspection and reflection and decides to take a plunge in the movement started by Gandhi—'I feel if I join one of Gandhi's non-violent campaigns, with pure heart and mind, and rid myself of fears, I may shape myself.' (533). He writes to Gandhiji for an appointment and keeps writing the story of Bakha for his novel. He shows his thesis to Bertrand Russell. The latter appreciates his efforts by saying

'I like your emphasis on imagination, empathy sympathy . . . It may be the only way out in a world where God is no more. Against despair, we must have the courage to live, and find out. . .' (563). By this time he receives a long admonishing letter from his father which forms the content of Part Eight. In this letter he is asked to come to see his ailing mother. The next part is a 'Letter to Father' in which he explains his position and tells what he thinks of his father. But he also feels inclined to visit home. Prof. Dicks approves his thesis and allows him to go for sometime. The last part is in the form of a letter to Irene informing her of his plans and his resolve to be a seeker after truth.

Though *The Bubble* is the latest novel of Anand, it is in the form of a record tracking Krishan's movements abroad. Written in a confessional mode, *The Bubble* is more than a confession, more even than an autobiography. Anand is not confused on the autobiographical element in a novel. He says, 'I have a hunch "all the characters in this novel are imaginary" is a lying phrase. There is no novel without real people. Only names are changed to avoid libel action." (165). It is a strong evidence of the maturity of the artist in a man who is capable of rising above the self, take out the self and look at himself in an objective way. It is also relevant to remember that Krishan has been much influenced by the humanism of Iqbal and he goes to England with the objective of exploring "the concept of self in the Philosophy of Muhammad Iqbal: how man can transform himself if he wants to, with his will.'(3) For Anand, therefore, it makes no difference if he narrates his experiences in the name of Krishan. Because, to him the truth and its analysis are more important than the garb of the experimenter and his tools. He is also conscious about the role of the writer and the importance of his writings. He records in his diary at Parsonage, Dolgelly, North Wales, 21.12.1925, that "All creative writing is thus a performance.

One recalls memories. One relates them to the present. One takes them to the depth of one's being. And one dramatises oneself in expression, so that the reader may say: 'Oh' I felt like that,!' Thus, Anand is not merely writing a novel *The Bubble*, but is actually giving us a theory of fiction in the manner of Henry Fielding but in the style of Henry James. Though the novel is no direct explanation of the title, the spirit of the bubble pervades the whole scheme of it and we find the novelist is bursting forth with ideas and philosophy of a writer who has had more than his cup full of life. Prof. Rhys says,'Bubbles always burst'(168). Hence the title.

*The Bubble* is a valuable chunk mirroring the life of a novelist. It is full of crucial information on the role of Irene in shaping his life and ideas and sustaining him in his beliefs. There should be no doubt that Irene Rhys of *The Bubble* is the same daughter of Professor who was in intense love with the author and who actually promised to marry him if he published his book. However, the contribution of Irene in Krishan's development as a writer-philosopher-rebel is phenomenal. The facts of the flesh, her readiness to mate with anyone who dared is less offensive than Krishan's weakness for girls. For him any female is a game and the bitterness of the sweet memories lingers on only until some other one takes her predecessor's place. Thus, the bohemia of Krishan does not end with a Yasmeen or an Irene. For him Eltie Helman would be equally welcome, in fact, should be more welcome for her sincerity and devotion to the cause of communism. But apparently she seems desexualised by her devotion to the cause, hence not worth wasting time on. These matters are, however, not so important as his quest.. He had gone to England to study "the concept of self" and "how man can transform himself." He himself wonders, 'I have come to the West to learn philosophy but I find myself becoming a student of life.'(346).

The names of the protagonists of the novels *Confession of a Lover* and *The Bubble* are very significant. It is no coincidence that Krishan is a Punjabi pronunciation of Sanskrit Krishna—The Lord. We find Krishna in love with the Gopis wherever he goes, in the image of the lord wooed by the illusory Gopis. In England too, he is wooed by all the girls that come across him—Lotika, Evelyn, Lucy, Irene, Eltie.

Mulk Raj Anand sees fiction only as a means and not as an end in itself. For him it is a means by which he strikes at the evils prevalent in Indian society together with the perpetrators of the evil, chief of whom is the priesthood. The contemptuous attitude of Krishan in *Seven Summers; Morning Face; Confession of a Lover* and the submissiveness of Ananta in *The Road* as well as the sufferings of Bakha and Munoo, the protagonists of *Untouchable* and *Coolie* respectively are mostly due to the attitude of different people formed by religion and its ritual. Anand does not hide his contempt for the man-made God and is only too restless to let go of a chance to show it. The whole exercise of the fiction of Mulk Raj Anand is therefore, his revolt against the rotting social system that breeds all the ills including the degeneration of the Hindu race. Almost all the protagonists of Anand are, therefore, unheroic in their conduct and demeanour because their true manliness is contaminated by the poison of religion and its agents. They are just the victims and puppets in the complex social structure that revolves round the priesthood that in turn does not allow anyone to assert his or her worth. The imagination and the psyche of the nation is thus imprisoned and not even Prince Vicky is free from it. His weakness is not Ganga Dasi but a woman who is the daughter of a priest and hence has the support of the priesthood as a whole against which he neither has the courage to revolt nor the alternative. A ruler without the support of the priesthood is just a mad howler who is fit only to be condemned to a madhouse far away. Bakha meekly suffers because, to his knowledge and experience, existence outside the Brahmin dominated social structure is inconceivable. He runs away from Colonel Hutchinson because in him also he hears the echo of the tantrums of the priesthood. He does not feel much miserable after preaching of Gandhi that the brahmins may do the job of untouchables but the sweeping and sweepers cannot be removed. Munoo's whole life is tragic because he is not a brahmin. If he were, he would not be assaulted at the public tap while in the employ of Mrs. Nathoo Ram. If he were a brahmin, anybody would have kept him as Prabha does keep Munoo as his own son.

The tragedy of Gauri is no different from the tragedy of Bakha and Munoo because a woman is the weakest member of the society. She lives by the strength of the male and is thoroughly exploited by him both physically and emotionally. In the case of Gauri, the male support behind her is not only weak but doubtful. Her foster father Amru is interested in selling and reselling her. Her husband Panchi is so weak that he cannot keep her to himself and has to send her back to her parents in the times of crisis when his crop fails due to drought and the character assassination of Gauri at the hands of his aunt Kesaro is at its peak. She should be a harbinger of good luck and prosperity. If she fails to be a good woman, she should better be banished, sold and considered an object fit to be sexually exploited. There is no use for a woman in Indian society that does not fit in either of the above roles. Gauri is, therefore, the rightful claimant to Anand's attention and sympathetic treatment.

In a system based on feudal notions of religion, wealth and muscle power, all those who do not possess one of these have to live on the mercy of this triumvirate. Even within this triumvirate, there is a constant struggle to gain supremacy by one over the other. But, in the times of danger to one from any force outside of these, they tend to unite to crush the common danger. That is why Harnam Singh, the zamindar of Anantpur and Seth Chaman Lal, the moneylender, are always supported by the British officers and the government machinery, including police. They are allowed maximum latitude to perpetrate injustice and indulge plunder so long as they are loyal and subservient to them. For the same reason, Count Rampal Singh of Rajgarh (*Sword and Sickle*) is out of favour with the British because he has apparently aligned himself with the revolutionaries and the followers of Gandhi. The fate of Gangu is worse because he not only resists his exploitation and that of his daughter but also he does not belong to one of the categories of the triumverate.

Any Indian, particularly Hindu, who has neither the power of muscle nor that of money, nor is he a member of the priest class is, therefore, at a disadvantage in the social hierarchy. He is fit to be exploited, abused and cast aside. The tragedy of these people is that in spite of realisation of their weak position, they are disunited. They would rather fight among themselves for establishing their own superiority than unite and fight their common enemies. There is an inbuilt mechanism in the social system that facilitates segregation and encourages alienation of one from the rest. The protagonists of Anand, therefore, represent this dismal aspect of the personality of Indian masses who can never be heroic in the conventional sense. They can only suffer. But, innumerable pulls start operating upon them, the moment they explore the possibility of retaliation. Their heroism is sapped and pawned not by their own acts and doings but by the very system in which they are born. They are neither dummies nor are they automatons. They feel and experience. They are capable of analysing the situation and deciding upon a course of action. Bakha feels like slapping back the merchant on the road as well as the priest, who tries to molest his sister.

This is because he is assured of whatever place he has in the social hierarchy. In sharp contrast with Bakha is the plight of Munoo who can never think of resisting or protesting against any injustice or cruelty. It is because his very existence is endangered in the absence of a place and that of any means to support him. Except Munoo, all the other protagonists of Anand are better placed because all of them have their lands even though heavily mortgaged and, a place called home where they can always go back. Munoo alone is a solitary figure being tossed from corner to corner and margin to margin in search of roots and consequent identity. He is the weakest spot in the chain of protagonists also because all his efforts are directed towards eeking a subsistence. He is allowed no time to think of setting up his own home and plan for his future because his present itself is an enigma to him. Bakha, Gangu, Lal Singh, Gauri, Krishan—all of them have a future to which they can look irrespective of whether they can make it or want or don't want to make it. Munoo alone is a lost soul for whom life has no other meaning than to secure some crumbs to fill his belly and spread the limb when exhausted—an existence no better and no different from that of the denizens of the forest.

Munoo thus, is a big question mark in the queue of Anand's creations in which each of them seems asking an altogether a different riddle. If the riddle of Munoo is whether man's whole life's purpose is to work day and night like a beast of burden so as to earn only a few crumbs not enough to fill one's belly at a time, then Bakha queries whether man is bound by or can create his own destiny. Whether he is a born slave to conventions or is any latitude granted him to devise and work up his own life. Gangu stares us in the face as if asking if alternatives are only for special being? Have the dispossessed and bonded no alternative but to live and behave as prescribed by and as pleases their masters. And, Gauri, the eternally abused woman, has the ages old dilemma of whether Sita will continue to be turned out of her own house with stigma by those who have no right; and no business to do so. Krishan alone is Anand's answer to these riddles and queries and dilemmas. He will not care to feed sadhus and priests and peers in exchange for their worthless blessings and prescriptions. Neither would he allow himself to be abused, blackmailed and sold by the so called guardians. He would have their love if offered but would not care for their contempt and hatred whether it comes from his own people and co-religionists or the so called non-believers like Muslims and Christians. He does not attach importance to the false notions of purity and impurity on the basis of vegetarian or non-vegetarian meals or Hindu or Muslim touch. He would rather marry Mumtaz, the courtezan, and be happy, than marry ignorant and narrowminded Draupadi from his own community and allow his life to be made a hell as happens to his brother Harish.

He would not succumb to the tyrannical dictates even though of his own father who has his own notions of prestige and prosperity. He would rather break free of these chains, the bonds of maya and moha, and go to distant England from where he would have a re-look at himself, his past and the world in which he grew. He would not love some girl whimsically selected by his parents for momentary gains of money and jewellery in total disregard of the aspirations and suitability of temperament, for each other.

Krishan is Anand's promise. He is the sole answer to all the problems raised in his fiction. He is sociable and amiable towards everybody. He would not be self-centred and narrow-minded, conventional and timid like Ganesh. He will allow no inhibitions to overtake him. Rather, he would overawe everything and everybody. He would see the world through the eyes of love and feel through the throbbing heart of love. It would be immaterial whether these eyes and hearts are going to be those of Hindu 'immoral' Devaki, or Muslim prostitute Mumtaz or the low class Christian Helen. It could be through the detached devotion of Irene Rhys. Krishan does not feel discouraged or thwarted in his march towards maturity and graduation. It may be in the interest of the system to isolate him but he would not allow it to happen to himself. Krishan's alienation from his parents and motherland is voluntary and brought about by himself. No external forces are responsible for this state of his being. Unlike other protagonists who are helpless witnesses of their distancing from their environment and people, Krishan has a purpose in seeking to alienate himself from all those around him. This he does with a view to attain total and unbiased objectivity so essential to seek the understanding of the self and the system of which one is a part. This cannot be possible so long as one continues to participate in the events. It was not advisable even for the ancient sages and learned men of India. They always preferred to retire to the denseness of forests farther and farther away from the daily temptations and demands of the ordinary world. But this had limited impact which is not approved by Anand because, to him 'to remain enclosed in the vicious circle of the old world, merely because some of us, saints and artists, had tasted the ultimate and enduring satisfactions of qualitative living?' (60) Krishan, the son of an ordinary head clerk in the vast network of the British Indian Army therefore, goes to England not so much to understand the West as to understand the east. Mulk Raj Anand has affirmed the imperative need of such an approach, in a letter to this author: 'it was my going away to the west that liberated me in many ways. And then the return home was liberation from the west,...'(Letter to the author, dated 21 Feb. 1986). Removing from the scene of actions is a good device to achieve that objectivity which confers rare distinction upon the worth and quality of a work of art. The tragedy of Bakha, Munoo, Gangu, Gauri, Lal Singh, Bhikhu, Ananta, Maqbool *et al.* is that they are offered no opportunity and facility to move away from the routine problems of life. They are helpless creatures devoid of the capacity to shake off their fetters and move other men and set trends. They are, thus, no heroes but faceless individuals representing the masses and their composition. However, collectively it is heroic.

The concerns of the fiction of Anand are unmistakable. He seems to be exercised over the destiny of India as a free nation. If its Bakhas, Munoos, Bhikhus, Gangus, Anantas, Maqbools, Lalus and Gauris are denied hope and repairment then it should be very depressing and disastrous for the young nation as a whole. It raises fundamental questions of fate of the Indian polity if improvement in the lot of these people is to be of no one's concern except that of poets like Iqbal! Where is the India of the dreams of Gandhi and Nehru going? Should it perpetuate the conventional pattern of life without offering any succour and hope for the down and out! The fault, according to Anand lies with what he calls the inhuman pattern of society as a whole and not with individuals irrespective of their higher or lower status. All of them are the victims of this pattern at one time or the other. But hardly any one of them tries to rise and think beyond the state of victimisation except Krishan. Evidently, therefore, Anand has reserved the role of an emancipated being for this hero of the series of his autobiographical novels, *Seven Summers, Morning Face, Confession of a Lover*, and *The Bubble*.

These four novels not only present a comprehensive account of the growth of Krishan from a childling to a fully mature adult but also trace the graph of graduation of his personality as a responsible and conscious being capable of deciding for himself in defiance of advice and expectations of forces representing conventions. This quartet can be considered as the modern Indian-epic in prose encompassing the trials and tribulations of the nation in the remaking. Together they present, a plan for India to be a just, equitable and assured social system, of a dream held fast through ages—the dream of Ram Rajya that every Indian cherishes a desire to realise and be a participant in.

Anand is not a Marxist by any definition, as occasionally branded. He is a humanist with positive faith in the existence of a Supreme Being guiding the destiny of mankind without discrimination on the basis of race, colour and not the least on the basis of man-made divisions of caste and untouchability. His protagonists including Krishan, the irrepressible trend setter, therefore, freely mix with whoever allows them to and eat and share their grievances without observing any taboos. They do not hate Muslims or Christians if they happen to be Hindus. The finest example of secularism is set by Maqbool Butt who refuses to be blinded by religious appelations and prefers to die for his faith in secular values that flourish better in India than in fanatically theocratic Pakistan. He is no Marxist also because a marxist denies the existence of God. In an *Apology for Heroism* he says "God (who) manifests Himself in the world process through Lila"(39) which can, by no stretch of imagination be interpreted as the negation or denial of God. He has unambiguously stated, however, his whole-hearted and total disapproval of priesthood that has devised elaborate ritual to exploit man in the name of God. The exploitation in the name of God is so extensive and intensive that it has bred corruption and denegration, moral and material both. Anand considers it a national stigma and a disease that has eaten the very marrow of the society to the extent that various limbs of the same body clatter against one another instead of working in unison. Various sections of Indian society have become vulnerable to the divisive policies and propaganda of the type echoed by Master Budh Singh before the boys; 'The sarkar is going to help all Muslims and Sikhs, who have been kept down by the Hindus— I will tell you this because I know! (*Morning Face* 267) The attitude of Budh Singhs is as painful to Anand as that of Ram Chands, Butas, Amrus, and Batras, Harnam Singhs, Chaman Lals, Suraj Manis and Sajnus, all of whom are, in their ignorances, weakening the roots of the giant society on the one hand while consciously colluding with external forces deeply interested in perpetuating their stranglehold on it. This state of affairs can be repaired only with the spread of education among the deprived and the dispossessed. Bakha, therefore, is portrayed as a claimant to all sympathy in his endeavour to seek educational enlightenment monopolised by the high castes which is invariably assured to him wherever he appears.

The fiction of Anand is also marked by buoyancy for a final redemption of the ever worsening human situation. It seeks to generate a hope for the triumph of good over evil as the only natural course possible. The good has not triumphed so far as his books are concerned but a very assuring note is struck in his 'Dedication' of *Morning Face*. He says, Krishan. . . . though I was to be your creator, you took control of the book, almost as if you were the author.' This is an admission of the triumphant quality of the force of goodness which needs no external regulation and is capable of charting its own course in order to spread and fertilise vast areas that are amenable to it. This basic goodness is what Anand wants to propound and contaminate everything around with it. Thus, he displays saintly qualities of seeing hope amidst darkness of evil; of not preaching hatred but believing in converting bad into good by love and understanding. He does not preach or pin his hopes on any type of external revolutions except a 'revolution in the consciousness of man' that alone may deliver mankind from its self created perils and paranoias.

The writing of Anand is marked by an intense desire to pay his debt to the mankind that sustained and supported him in his endeavour to look into the problems of existence.

The recurrence of the names like Munoo, Bakha, Gangu, Maqbool, Nur, Chhota, are those passing but sharp specks on the memory screen who have contributed to his growth as an artist and more than an artist as a sensitive observer of human predicament.

# Bibliography

*Untouchable* 1935

*Coolie* 1933

*Two Leaves and a Bud.* 1937

*The Village.* 1937

*Across the Black Waters.* 1940

*The Sword and the Sickle.* Bombay: Kutub Popular 1942

*The Big Heart.* 1945

*Seven Summers.* 1951

*Private Life of An Indian Prince.* 1953

*The Old Woman and the Cow Gauri,* 1960

*Lament on the Death of the Master of Arts.* 1967

*The Road.* 1961.

*Death of A Hero.* 1963.

*Morning Face.* 1961.

*Confession of a Lover, 1976*

*The Bubble.*

**Short Story Collections**

Anand, Mulk Raj. *The Lost Child and Other Stories.* London: J.A. Allen & Co. 1934.

*The Barber's Trade Union and others Stories.* Bombay: Kutub Popular, 1952.

*Indian Fairy Tales (Retold)*. Bombay: Kutub Popular, 1946.

*The Tractor and the Corn Goddess and Other Stories*. Bombay: Current Book House, 1954.

*Reflections on the Golden Bed and other Stories*. Bombay: Current Book House, 1954.

*Selected Stories*. Moscow: Foreign Language Publishing House, 1955.

*The Power of Darkness and Other Stories*. Bombay: Jaico Publishing House, 1959.

*Aesop's Fables (Retold)*, Bombay: Dhawale: Popular, 1960.

*More Indian Fairy Tales (Retold)*, Bombay: Kutub Popular, 1961.

*Lajwanti and other Stories*. Bombay: Jaico. 1966.

*Between Tears and Laughter*. New Delhi: Sterling Publishers, 1973.

*Folk Tales of Punjab*. New Delhi: Sterling, 1974.

**Articles:**

"Anglo-Saxon Attitudes: Twentieth Century English Fiction About India." *The Image of India in Western Creative Writing*. M.K. Naik, S.K Desai and ST Kallapur, Dharwar: Karnatak University Publications, 1971.

"The Changeling." *World Literature Written in English*. Vol. XV No. 1, April 1976.

"Creative Process." *Littcrit*. Vol. IV, No. 1, June 1978.

"Creative Writing in the Present Crisis." *Indian Literature*. Vol. VI. No. 1, 1963.

"Crossroads in Life." *Debonair*, Vol. V, No. 4, April 1976.

"How I Became A writer." *Mirror*, May 1977.

"Images and Words," *The Illustrated Weekly of India*. June 8, 1980.

"Is Universal Criticism Possible." *The Literary Criterion*. Vol. VII. No. 1, Winter 1965.

"Literature's Revolutionary Message." *Youth Times*. Oct. 28-Nov. 10, 1977.

"The Meaning of Words." *Mirror*. Sept. 1977.

"National Integration and Indian Creative Writers." *Indian Literature*. Vol. V, No. 1, 1962.

"Old Myths and New Myths—Recital Vs Novel." *The Banasthali Patrika*. No. 13, July 1969.

"On the Use of Epithets, Swear-words, Curses and Imprecations." *Litcrit*. Vol. II, No. 2, Dec. 1976.

"The One and the Many: Some Changing Social Patterns of New India." *International Magazine of Afro-Asian Affairs*. Vol. XVIII, No. 1, Jan_Feb 1966

"Pigeon English: Some Notes on Indian-English Writing." *Karnatak University Journal*, 1972.

"Pigeon English and Pigeon India." *Commonwealth Quarterly*. Vol. III, No. 10, March 1979.

"The Place of Art in University Education." *The Journal of University Education*. Vol. II, No. 1, Sept. 1963.

"The Place of Gifted Individual in Indian Society." *The Year Book of Education*. London: Evans Brothers Ltd., 1961.

"The Rhythms of Indian Life—On Indian English." *Research and Criticism*. Ed. N. Radhakrishan. Annamalai: Research Scholars' Association. 1975.

"The Story of My Experiment With a White Lie." *Critical Essays on Indian Writing in English*, Ed. MK Naik *et al.* Madras: Macmillan of India, 1968.

"Synthesis, Conflict of Experiment." *Eve's Weekly*. Aug. 20-26

"Trends in the Modern Indian Novel." *The Journal of Indian Writing in* English. Vol. I, No. 1, Jan. 1973.

"An Undeclared War." *Littcrit*. Vol. III, No. 1, June 1977.

"Why I Write." *Indo English Literature: A Collection of Critical Essays*. Ed. K.K. Sharma. Ghaziabad: Vimal Prakashan. 1977.

"Whither India?" *Gandhi Marg*. Vol. XI, No. 4, Oct. 1967.

"Writer's Role in Modern Society." *Contemporary Indian Literature*. Vol. IX, No. 1, Jan. 1969.

"The Writer's Role in National Integration: A Discussion." *Indian Literature*. Vol. V. No. 1, 1962.

### Secondary Sources

Rerry, Margaret, *Mulk Raj Anand The Man and the Novelist* Amsterdem: Oriental Press, 1971.

Cowasjee, Saros. *So Many Freedoms: A Study of the Major Fiction of Mulk Raj Anand*. Maaras University Press. 1977.

Gupta, Balaram G.S. *Mulk Raj Anand: A Study of His Fiction in Humanist Perspective*. Bareilly: Prakash Book Depot. 1974.

Sing, Satyanarayana. Ed. *Kakatiya Journal of English Studies: Mulk Raj Anand Special Number*. Vol. II, No. I, Spring 1977.

Lindsay, Jack. *The Elephant and the Lotus: A Study of the Novels of Mulk Raj Anand*. Bombay: Kutub-Popular. 1965.

Naik, M.K. *Mulk Raj Anand*. Delhi: Arnold Heinemann India, 1978.

Niven, Alastair. *The Yoke of Pity*. Delhi: Arnold Heinemann, 1978.

Sharma, K.K. *ed. Perspectives on Mulk Raj Anand*. Ghaziabad: Vimal Prakashan, 1978.

Reimenshneider, D. *An Ideal of Man in Mulk Raj Anand's Novels*. Bombay: Kutub-Popular, 1967.

Sinha, Krishna Nanadan, *Mulk Raj Anand*. New York: Twayne Publishers, 1972.

Abidi, SZH. *Mulk Raj Anand's Coolie: A Critical Study*. Bareilly: Prakash Book Depot, 1976.

Badal, RK, *Indo Anglian Literature: An Outline*, Bareilly: Prakash Book Depot. 1975.

Carter, D. "Probing Identities: Untouchable, Things Fall Apart and This Earth, My Brother...." *The Literary Criterion*. Vol. IV, No. 33, 1979.

Chginneswararao, G.J. "Anand's Private Life and Malgaonkar's Princes." *The Journal of Indian Writing in English*. Vol. IV, No. 1, Jan. 1976.

Cowasjee, Saros, "Anand's Literary Creed." *The Journal of Indian Writing in English*. Vol. I, Jan. 1973.

———, "Anand's Princes and Proletarians." *The Literary Half-Yearly*. Vol. IX, No. 2, 1968.

———, "Anand's Two Leaves and a Bud." *Indian Literature*. Vol. XVI. Nos. 3&4, Jul.-Dec. 1973.

———, "*The Big Heart:* A New Perspective." *ACLALS Bulletin* No. 2, 1975.

———, *Coolie: An Assessment*. Delhi: Oxford Univ. Press. 1976.

———, "Mulk Raj Anand's The Sword and the Sickle." *World Literature Written in English*. Vol. XIV, No. 2, Nov. 1975.

———, "Mulk Raj Anand's *Untouchable:* An Appraisal." *Indo English Literature: A Collection of Critical Essays*. KK Sharma. ed. Ghaziabad: Vimal, 1977.

———, "Princes and Politics." *The Literary Criterion*. Vol. III, No. 4, 1969.

———, "Review of Margaret Berry's *Mulk Raj Anand: The Man and the Novelist;* Amesterdem: Oriental Press, 1971.

Dutt, Prabhat Kumar. "Mulk Raj Anand in Relation to Tagore, Premchand and Sarat Chatterjee." *Contemporary Indian Literature*. Vol. V, Nos. 11&12, Nov-Dec. 1965.

Fisher, Mariene. "Mulk Raj Anand's Confessional Novels." *The Journal of Indian Writing in English.* Vol. IV, No. 2, July 1976.

———, "Mulk Raj Anand: The Novelist as Novelist." *Punjab University Research Bulletin,* April 1973.

———, "The Shape of Lostness: Mulk Raj Anand's Short Stories." *The Journal of Indian Writing in English.* Vol. II, No. 1, Jan. 1974.

Gowda, Anniah H.H. "Mulk Raj Anand." *The Literary Half-Yearly.* Vol. VI, No. 1, Jan. 1965.

Gupta, Balarama G.S. "Anand's Big Heart: A Study" *Banasthali Patrika,* July *1965.*

———, "Anand's Old Woman and the Cow in Humanist Perspective," *Karnataka University Journal.* Vol. XIV., 1970.

———, "Woman in Anand's Shorter Fiction." *Karnataka U.J.,* Vol. XIII, 1969.

Hemenway, Stephen, *Mulk Raj Anand: The Novel of India.* Vol. II. Calcutta: Writers Workshop, 1975.

Henderson, Philip. *Mulk Raj Anand: The Novel Today.* London: The Bodley Head, 1936.

# R.K. Narayan

Rasipuram Krishnaswami Narayan was born on 10th October 1906 to R.V. Krishnaswami Iyer and Gnanambal at Purasawalkam, Madras. It was a congested, noisy and dusty downtown locality. The large family of Iyers included several uncles, brothers, sisters and cousins. Narayan himself was the third of eight children of his parents. The household included grandmothers and grandfathers on both mother's and father's side besides grand uncles and aunts because of the practice of intermarriage between the sister's and brother's children. Narayan himself was looked after more by his maternal grandmother addressed as Ammani rather than by his own mother. Because of closeness with the Wodeyars, the rulers of Mysore State, his father took up service as a teacher in Maharaja's School. The School was later upgraded as Maharaja's collegiate High School and his father was made its Principal. The Tamil speaking Iyer brahmins, thus, came to Kannada homeland of Mysore. Though his other brothers could assimilate Kannada culture-traits in their bearing and thinking, Narayan could not, somehow, naturalise himself as a Kannadiga. Sociologist Srinivas says, "Narayan's formative years were in Madras. He came from an Iyer family in Madras, as a middleclass family. And he remained that throughout his life even though he spent the major part of his life in Mysore. But he doesn't see Kannada culture as a Kannadiga does. He is external to Karnataka."[1]

He was not much interested in studies. He had a dread of Mathematics and mechanical contrivances. Besides, he suffered regular persecution and humiliation as the only Brahmin student at E.L.M. Fabricius School, Purasawalkam. Here the students and teachers were mostly converted Christians who spared no opportunity to denigrate Hindu gods and practices with "a somewhat proselytizing attitude towards its non-Christian students."[2] After his graduation from Maharaja's College, Mysore he was widely advised and urged to study English Literature for M.A. But, he finally decided against it although he did read Carlyle, Ruskin, Fielding, Thackeray and Sir Walter Scott besides European and Greek classics in English translation.[3] In the recommendation and standing of his father, he taught at Maharaja's College for some time. However, he left in owing to several problems of stay and work. He walked out with the determination not to take up teaching as a career.

After forsaking teaching, he declared his resolve to be a writer: "I thought I would throw myself full time in this gamble of a writer's life."[4] As a consequence of this resolve he associated himself with *The Justice,* the mouthpiece of the South Indian Liberal Federation set up in 1916 around Non-Brahmin Manifesto. The movement was better known as the Justice Party. To begin with, Narayan was content with being a stringer. However, his first anonymously published piece was a review of Development of Maritime Laws of 17th Century England. The first piece of writing for which he received a handsome payment of ten rupees was his short story, 'A Night in a Rest House' published in *The Indian Review*, August 1932. Next year saw him achieving a great breakthrough in the publication of his short piece, 'How to write an Indian Novel," in *Punch* (London: Sept. 1933). He was thus launched on a writing career with the patronizing help of famous British novelist Graham Greene. On the recommendation of the latter, Hamish Hamilton published his first novel *Swami and Friends*

(1935). Thereafter appeared *The Bachelor of Arts* (1937); *The Dark Room*, ('38); *The English Teacher* (1945); *Mr. Sampath—The Printer of Malgudi* (1949); *The Financial Expert* (1952); *Waiting for the Mahatama* (1955); *The Guide* (1958); *The Man-Eater of Malgudi* (1962); *The Vendor of Sweets* (1967); *The Painter of Signs* (1976); *A Tiger for Malgudi* (1983); *Talkative Man* (1986); *The World of Nagaraj* (1990); *The Grandmother's Tale: Three Novellas* (1993). His other books include, autobiographies: *My Days: A Memoir* (1974): *My Dateless Dairy: An American Journey* (1964); Short story collections: *Malgudi Days* (1943); *Dadu and Other Stories* (1943); *Cyclone and Other Stories* (1945); *An Astrologer's Day and Other Stories* (1947); *Lawley Road and Other Stories* (1956); *A House and Two Goats* (1970); *Malgudi Days* (1982); *Under the Banyan Tree and Other Stories* (1985); Miscellaneous: *Next Sunday; Sketches and Essays* (1956); *Reluctant Guru* (1974); *A Writer's Nightmare: Selected Essays* (1988); *A Story Teller's World* (1989); *Salt and Sawdust: Stories and Table Talk* (1993); Travellogues: *Mysore* (1939); *The Emerald Route* (1977). *Folklore and Epics Retold: Gods, Demons and Others* (1964); *The Ramayana* (1972); *The Mahabharatu* (1978); *The Indian Epics Retold* (1995). He also edited the three issues of the first volume of the journal *Indian Though* (1941). Besides, his stray articles, reviews, skits and the one-act-play "Everest" have appeared in *Indian Review, The Merry Magazine, The Madras Mail, Punch, The Times of India, The Illustrated Weekly of India,* from 1932.

*Keep These Facts in Mind when considering the work of R.K. Narayan :*

The Southern half of India is surrounded by the seas on all the sides. The western edge is lapped up by the Arabian Sea while the eastern edge is marked by the Bay of Bengal and the southern most tip enters the Indian ocean. The upper India is geographically secured by Vindhyachal ranges with a 'buffer' called the Deccan plateau. To the far-far south-east lies the rock of Australia and no formidable lands to its south-west. The South India has, thus, been a God's secure region for all intent and purposes. Kings and religious missionaries have been known to venture off eastern coast rather than any adventurers landing in. There have been no invasions and no assaults from the north and all those who invaded the north felt satisfied with ambitions exhausted by reaching the Vindhyas. The mighty Moguls also left the south undisturbed and the north Indian men of might like Chandragupta and Ashoka would have no concept of their empires extending to the Cape Camorin (Kanyakumari). This gave the south to rule itself according to its pleasure, and lead life according to its whim and fancy. The society in the south has, therefore, a different frame of mind. In the absence of external dangers, it has ample leisure to indulge internal squabbles and worry about minor but finer detail. The external invader has no regard for tradition and values of the native. He not only plunders but destroys too. Women are coveted most by invaders. However, internal strifes and neighbourhood expeditions, civilians were not harmed and destruction and plunder were limited to royal treasures and property. The south India therefore, offered maximum liberty to the woman so much so that it developed into is female-centric. The woman in the South is more secure, more independent, more respected and plays a dominant role in family and society. However, her concerns remain largely feministic: marriage, property and share in family assets, pampering of children and the like issues become more prominent. Petty gossip and temple related activities are the major preoccupations, therefore, in the narratives from the south. Caste becomes a cause of great agitation and gold the biggest obsession.

In the novels of R.K. Narayan, we find the above concerns at various levels and in many dimensions. His most charming creation—the town of Malgudi—reverberates with the shouts of joy and fun indulged in by children. It is a town with all the typical characteristics of a south Indian town. Life centres round the temple and ordinary establishments become prominent focal points of activity. One is led to wonder what would be happening elsewhere! People are god-fearing and anyone deviating from the norms would be a monster. There is faith reposed by one in the other and betrayal of trust would be taken cognition of by gods. Divine punishment must visit every wrong doer. However, the status based on official position and personal wealth is a crucial factor in the south Indian society too. The official position dictates one's attitude and conduct vis-a-vis the other. The social status draws its strength from another factor: One's connection with the western countries. Visit to England, either for acquiring educational qualification or for vacationing is sure to enhance one's prestige in the society and the community. It instils a sense of superiority in the beneficiary and a corresponding sense of inferiority among the satellites.

Aligned to this England-returned aspect is the factor of Brahminism. Only 'superior caste' people deserve education in England. Here, the Gandhian concern of vegetarianism does not cause any stir. That is a non-issue. However, untouchability is a major issue in the south. The lower castes must live separately from the upper castes and distantly too. The socio-economic status must also be reflected in the architecture and storeys of the residence. Ordinary visitors must be dealt with on the open platform outside the main entrance and the low caste must not dare climb it. Horoscope is sacrosanct and must be taken seriously because it is also a work of divine scholarship, reserved only for the Brahmin.

The above scenario is visible in *The Bachelor of Arts*. Chandran is the elder son of a retired District Judge. His classmates offer him precedence in all the matters of extra curricular activities like debates, office of secretary of Historical Association, reading papers. Unlike an ordinary student, he is not in a hurry to look for a job or even to prosecute higher studies. Instead he falls in love with a girl of a low level employee. To add to the sufferings of young Chandran, his horoscope does not match with that of the girl. This is a very insurmountable obstacle because ignoring this mismatch would be inviting the wrath of gods in heaven.

The theme of social status dominates the narrative of *Swami and Friends*. Swaminathan is a back bencher in great contrast with Rajam who dominates the scene since the day of his arrival. This is because he has all the facilities like a separate study room at home, lots of money to spend on friends. He has status of being the son of Superintendent of Police. Being the son of an ordinary person he is easily targeted as a mischief-maker and expelled from the prestigious school. Though dull, he realises the low quality of teaching and atmosphere at the new School. His inferiority complex further comes to the fore when he cannot express his feeling on the parting of Rajam although both had been great friends and team-mates of the old school.

Savitri's plight in the *Dark Room* highlights the denial of human dignity to a woman in an arranged marriage. The male's affront gets an edge when he is the boss in the office and has the facility to appoint females around him. With the passage of age the wife's position becomes weaker and weaker. But in an Indian social situation a sensible husband would not like to precipitate disruption of domestic harmony over trivial matters, becomes even the private life is observed and commented upon by the neighbour as well as the society at large.

Belief in the spirit and life after death is pivotal to Indian's existence. One may be an English teacher by profession but his essential Indianness leaps out at every conceivable opportunity. So, Krishnan, the English teacher, can communicate with the spirit of his late wife. The story also highlights the superstitious belief of some supernatural power being present in the dirty toilet of a long forsaken house, only to claim Susila's life in order to prove the prediction based upon her horoscope. Another aspect of lower middle class India is presented in *Mr. Sampath-The Printer of Malgudi.* A Hindi speaker optimist Sampath helps Srinivas the South Indian youngman, start a weekly magazine *The Banner.* He edits, composes, prints, brings finances and introduces innovations to make the magazine a success. The magazine, in due course, becomes an agent of redressal of public grievances and improvement of civic facilities. He does it in great public spirit. Later, when revenues fail and cause the collapse of the magazine, he starts another highly ambitious venture of film production. He wants to produce films based on sexy themes, in preference to mythological themes. This deviation causes the collapse of this company too and drives home the message that the south Indian quetitude, piety of conduct and thought, and modest life style take a man along the path longer than the fast northern ways. This message is further strengthened in the story of *Financial Expert* that demonstrates that the ordinary people place their trust easily and withdraw it faster because it is always in pursuit of financial and material gains. They can raise a mortal to heights and drag him down to the gutter, once they get the wind of foul play. This is a very unconventional pointer to the working of democracy in India, where images rise by day and fall by nights. This is more amply and powerfully seen in the example of Raju, the Guide. It is the public reposition of faith that compels him to act and die a holyman even though he had no inclination towards either option. Raju is both an Indian enigma and a key to the mystery and myth. Here a man has lesser claim to his privacy. He lives more for others and is guided by external considerations and compulsions and is deified in spite of his disinclination and indifference. In great contrast to this are Vasus who are demonic in acts, conduct and concepts. Such people make life hell for simple law-abiding, humane folk and are kept in check by swamis who have disciplined their thought, desires and speech. If there are unleashed tigers like Vasu who would like to devour anyone and everyone, then there are Swamis too who would not be afraid of their monstrosities. Once we strengthen faith in ourselves by understanding the other, no harm will come to either of the two. The essence of Indian thought, philosophy and vision is contained in the narrative of *A Tiger for Malgudi,* therefore, that illustrates the harmonious view of several seemingly irreconcilable aspects of our existence. This was embodied by Mahatma Gandhi in a simpler but inexplicable form. Its elaboration is provided in the utterances of the ascetic. It is the large corps of ascetics that keeps so many diversities under check and balance and unite them into a creamy weave that is India.

# 'Swami and Friends'

*Swami and Friends* (1935) takes us to the world of school going children. Swaminathan is a student of First Form at Albert Mission School at Malgudi. He is a backbencher and one of the dull boys at studies. He has for friends equally dull boys like Mani, Samuel the Pea and a couple of brilliant ones too, like Somu the monitor and Sankar. A little later another very brilliant boy Rajam joins the group of Swami's friends. Mani is a bully with a wooden club is his dreaded weapon. After Rajam comes, however, he establishes his superiority over Mani in every respect. He is the son of the Police Superintendent and has facilities like separate study-room, an air-gun, servants to dance in attendance. After initial resistance on the part of Mani, Rajam establishes himself the leader with his friendly nature and material bounty. Soon after the arrival of Rajam, Swami's other friends desert him and attach themselves like a trail to Rajam. But Swaminathan is not shaken, and his friendship with Mani thickens. He and Mani visit Rajam and Rajam visits him. They play innocent games and chatter freely. Rajam, on his part, brings Swami's estranged friends closer, gives a lecture on friendship and also offers prizes.

At the approach of examinations all of them become serious. There is a general business-like reserve. Mani too starts consulting Sankar and other brilliant boys and haunts the residence of the school clerk for question-paper leakage. Swami too becomes serious and prepares a list of stationary items needed for preparations for examinations. Swami feels relieved at the end of the examinations and together with Rajam and Mani he loiters along the banks of Saryu and in the streets of Malgudi throughout the day. Very soon his absences are noticed and his father Srinivasan, a lawyer, also on his holidays because of closure of courts for the summer, takes him to task But Swami manages to rouse his grandmother and mother, by turns, to champion the cause of his truancy.

Once a tongawalla befooled Swami and obtained six pice thrice in the name of turning them into silver. When his friends Rajam and Mani came to know, they thought of avenging but the son of the tongawalla befooled Mani and ran away with his top before Mani could realise. Likewise Swami, Mani and Rajam have fun at the cost of a bullock-cartdriver boy whom they impress with their authority.

At the re-opening of the school, all the three find themselves promoted to the next higher grade. But, on 15th August 1930 Swami finds himself amidst the crowd outside the school, protesting against the Congress satyagrahi Gauri Shankar's arrest in Bombay. Swami sees an excellent opportunity to pelt stones at the window panes of the Headmaster's room. The next day, he is punished and expelled from the school. He is, however, admitted in the other school—Board High School, which is not as good as the Albert Mission School. Students here are given more home work and have to drill at school after four-thirty. The school's late-schedule irritates Swami and his friends at Albert Mission School who had formed themselves into a cricket club. Swami feels bitter at having been cut off from his old set. Rajam and Mani feel unhappy with Swami and his new school because they are free to practise after four-thirty but Swami does not get his release despite frantic efforts by his friends. Their team M.C.C. has fixed a match with the team of Y.M.U. and Swami has to be their dependable bowler. In order to seek his release from the Drillmaster after four-thirty Swami says that he suffers from delirium and also goes to a doctor Kesavan to obtain a certificate recommending his release. The plan misfires and the Headmaster beats Swami with his stick. Swami, however, throws the stick out of the window and runs away. The fact of losing this school gets the better of him and he suffers because there is no other school in Malgudi. He realises his future is bleak now. He is torn between his intense desire to play the match and his inability to face his parents. He wanders on the road to Mampi Hills and loses sense of the may back may home. With the help of a kind hearted cartman Ranga and a Forest Officer M P S Nair, he is restored to his parents. The match is lost, however, in the absence of Swami. Soon Rajam too leaves Malgudi with his parents since his father has been transferred to Trichinopolly. Much scared, he goes to see his friend off at the station early in the morning but fails to gather courage to talk to Rajam. His friend Mani, however, helps him and hands over his present, a book, to Rajam.

# 'The Bachelor of Arts'

*The Bachelor of Arts* (1937) is the story of Chandran. He is the elder of the two sons of a retired District judge. He belongs to a respectable family and is reading for his B.A. degree in the local Alberts College. He is a smart student and a good speaker. He is asked by his friend Natesan, the Secretary of the College Union to speak on the subject," Historians should be slaughtered first", because no one else is prepared to be the Prime Mover of the subject of the debate. Principal Brown in the Chair is much impressed of his talent and he is declared the winner. This encourages him to be bold at home too. He casually asks for his father's permission to go to the night-film-show with his friend Ramu and finds his otherwise strict father allows him to go to see the film.

Just when Chandran decides to devote himself to his studies, after taking part in extra curricular activities, his history professor Raghavachar asks him to form the Historical Association and nominates him its Secretary. Chandran seeks the help of everybody and formulates elaborate plans for its inauguration. The inauguration is a tremendous success compared to his first debate before about a score of boys hustled by Natesan. Thereafter he conducts about eight meetings of Historical Association and reads a paper on "The Lesser-known Aspects of Mauryan Polity." His schedule for studies has suffered because of his involvement with Historical Association. But after its inauguration, he imposes iron-discipline upon himself and rises at 4.30 in stead of at 5 in the morning to make up for the lost time.

Since he belongs to well-to-do parents, he is not in a hurry either to prosecute higher studies or to look for a job after passing his examination. Within six months of his becoming a graduate, however, he is faced with queries about his future plans. His parents are in a mood to send him to England to study for a doctorate. At about this time, he sees a girl Malathi, playing with her small baby-charge on the banks of Saryu one day. He immediately falls in love with her at first sight without any encouragement or reciprocation from her. He compels his parents to negotiate his marriage with that girl, although she is the daughter of a Head Clerk in the Chief Engineer's Office—much below the status of Chandran's family. Unfortunately the marriage is denied because the horoscopes of the two do not match. This is a great shock to Chandran and he is sent to his uncle in Madras instead of going to his uncle, he goes to a hotel. There he meets Kailas, who has made a lot of money in Malaya and keeps two wives, comes to Madras to drink wine and visit prostitutes. Chandran runs away from him and sleeps on the pavement. The next day he gives away all his money to a barber in exchange for shaving his head and for procuring him ochre coloured loin cloth. For about eight months he wanders about near and far places as an ascetic. One day, the people of a village gather around him to request him to permanently stay on in their village. He is alarmed and runs away, seeking and getting free ride in a lorry, to Maduram. He tells his story to the much scared post-master and borrows a rupee and eight annas for sending a telegram home for money.

After reaching home, he is received well. He wants to seek a government jot. But his father is again in a mood to send him to England. His friend Mohan, however, tells him of the possibility of getting the agency to the newspaper, *Daily Messenger* for Malgudi. He seeks prospects in this work and informs his father. With the influence of his uncle in Madras, he is appointed agent for the *Daily Messenger*. He opens an office and works hard from 8 in the morning to 8 in the night. From a mere 25, he promotes its sale to hundreds by adopting a systematic and enlightened approach. His good manners and knack for social connections help him succeed everywhere. Once again, the issue of his marriage crops up. But this time his friend Mohan's advice and his own matter of fact worldly wise attitude help him steer clear of sentimental confusion. He goes to see the girl Susila and atonce falls for her. After his marriage, his impatience for his wife's letters overcomes him again.

*The Bachelor of Arts* is a typical sentimental comedy. In the life of an ordinary Indian marriage is a high priority issue. If the head of the family holds a responsible and dignified position in the government, then the children must be destined to go to England for education. The young men, however, must fall in love at that age and must behave in accordance with the great tradition of Indian princes and heroes. In a typical South Indian Brahmin household the horoscope is a serious business and the horoscopes of the two must match. If it does not happen, then it is considered that god's approval is missing and no one dare go against it. Morality in public and private lives is maintained as a matter of course. Boozing and womanising are shunned and no one should be seen close to such persons. Chandran, therefore, runs away from Kailas even though he has no other place for refuge. However, Chandran's renunciation of the world by shaving his head and putting on ochre coloured clothes is unusual for his age. He himself does not agree with his ascetic status and returns home the moment he realises that he had made himself into one.

The novel is realistic in tone and is a mild commentary on parental whims about what their children should do and become. The tragedy of most of the households is that parents cultivate fancy notions and strange whims about the career of their children. In most of the cases parents want their children to become what they would have liked to become themselves and achieve that which they failed to achieve. In this planning the aptitude of the progeny, his liking and ambition are never ascertained and taken into account. Children are never asked what subjects they want to study or what they want to become. More often than not, the son has talent for something held in contempt or not in esteem by the father. This results in enormous waste of resources and precious time of life of a youngman who would work wonders otherwise.

The objective of the novelist in *The Bachelor of Arts* has been unambiguously demonstrated in the success of Chandran as a newspaper agent. It is surely a great setback to his father who visualised a civil service career and a girl from an established upper class family for his son. However, Chandran sees high prospects in an ordinary business and settles for Susila as his bride without being sentimental about the notion of high and low.

The story of *The Bachelor of Arts* is plain and its plot is simple. It seeks to record the workings of the mind of college going youth. No intricacies are involved. But at times it provides a lot of humour and ludicrousness as when Chandran and his father catch hold of the sanyasi who jumps over the locked gate to steal flowers at 4 in the morning because he concludes that he alone would be making the best use of them by offering them in worship to gods. Or, when Chandran reaches Madras station, after disappointment in marriage with Malathi, he slips his cousin and goes to stay in a hotel where, very soon he slips away from Kailas at the prostitute's place. Chandran is a highly talented and virtuous person. He is unorthodox in his views on all aspects of life. Horoscope, dowry, status do not mean anything to him and he easily persuades his parents to ignore them. The lure of going to England for higher education too does not work on him. He

The fruit and vegetable garden was under the care of a Japanese gardener until a few years ago, when he died prematurely. In his death the Institute suffered an irreparable loss. He was a perfect example of industry and hard work, and succeeded in raising all kinds of vegetables on a piece of land declared by agricultural experts to be absolutely unfit for growing vegetables. People from long distances came to see his garden, and were amazed at the beautiful crops and large variety of Indian, English, Japanese and Chinese vegetables.

Many of the health problems will be solved when vegetables and small-fruit growing can be successfully introduced in the villages. Very few people in Bengal are strict vegetarians; fish is the favourite meat diet. In West Bengal, however, due to the scarcity of rain, and consequently the high price of fish, the mass of the people cannot afford to include either meat or fish in their daily diet.

It is the purpose of the Institute to introduce vegetable gardening in every village family, so that they may improve their health through their diet without any additional cost.

**Dairy**

The condition of the dairy industry in Bengal is deplorable almost beyond description. It is particularly so in West Bengal. The obvious reason is scarcity of fodder. As a result the cattle are small, emaciated, and seem hardly to have any life at all. Even during the rainy season, when in other parts of India there is plenty of grazing to be had, in this part of Bengal there is only an inch or two of grass to be found on the lands where these cattle are allowed to graze. How these cattle manage to exist at all during the greater part of the year is most surprising, for they certainly seem to spend all their energy in going round all day trying to find a tuft of grass here and a tuft there; and yet at home they would be lucky if they were given a sheaf or two of rice-straw, a roughage of very poor quality. As for concentrates, they rarely have any; only the working bullocks are so fortunate, during the ploughing season, when their work is extremely heavy.

Under such conditions it is little wonder that the cattle are so poor and do not yield milk. On the average, a cow in full milk yields about a pint of milk per day. Other cows of the same size and breed, if well cared for and properly fed, yield as much as four to six quarts per day.

As regards breeding, on account of the ignorance and superstitious ideas and customs of the people, no systematic or scientific system is carried on. Diseased, old and utterly useless bulls are allowed to go about freely with the cows, and there is strong prejudice on the part of the Hindu cattle-breeders against castration.

The object of the dairy at the Institute is also twofold: (1) to supply both Sriniketan and Santiniketan with fresh, pure milk; and (2) to breed cattle, not only at the Institute, but to induce the cultivators to follow the scientific and systematic system of breeding, so that they may have not only good milch cows but also sturdy draught animals.

Cattle-breeding is the foundation of Indian agriculture, and will remain so for a long time to come, and yet very little attention has been paid to the improvement of cattle. The Government has a number of cattle-breeding farms, but so far the people have not taken advantage of them, not in Bengal at least. Very forceful propaganda is needed, and people have to be educated so that they may overcome their superstitions. Only then can this most important industry be improved.

So far as the production of milk is concerned, perhaps it would be more advisable to improve the goats, for they can always find some sort of grazing among shrubs and bushes on which the cows could not thrive. Whatever it may be, the goat or the cow, it is very essential that something should be done so that the people may have milk.

Efforts are being made to raise fodder and to show the cultivators its importance; but here it is not possible to do very much, since the amount of land which the average cultivator possesses is barely enough to raise foodstuffs for his family.

**Poultry**

In India little or no attention is given to the poultry industry. This could be very profitable, even as a subsidiary industry. Religious prejudices do not allow most of the cultivators to keep poultry; only the Mohammedans and the low-caste people are free from these prejudices. On account of lack of selection in breeding the laying capacity of the hens is extremely small. On the average an Indian hen lays from thirty to forty eggs per year. As regards feeding, the people spend nothing on feeds; the birds pick what they can find in the fields or in the heaps of rubbish lying about in the village. There are certain Indian breeds, however, which do lay more eggs of a fairly large size. If these hens were systematically and scientifically bred they could be developed into very good fowls, suited to the climate of the country.

The poultry section, while trying to introduce better breeds into the villages, also trains a number of apprentices. So far, all the apprentices have come from high castes, most of them college men, who intend to start poultry farms of their own. A few have already begun their work and are making good at it. The poultry farm, in addition to introducing the Chittagongs, one of the best Indian breeds, has imported some White Leghorns and Rhode Island Reds, and experiments are being carried on to test the suitability of the breeds for the local conditions. Experiments have also been made in crossing the village hens with White Leghorn cocks, and the results have been very encouraging. In a few villages, after inducing the people to get rid of their cocks, some Leghorn and Chittagong cocks have been distributed. The results are being watched with great interest.

## INDUSTRIES

Under the old village system, some of which is still to be found in parts of India, there is a distinction between the village menial and the independent artisan. Under the former, in descending order of respectability of trades, may be listed barbers, carpenters, weavers, blacksmiths, tanners, laundrymen and scavengers—the last three being considered as belonging to very low castes. Under the heading of independent artisans may be put down, in the same order, goldsmiths, potters, oilmen, tailors and dyers.

People belonging to the first groups were paid in kind—a share from the harvest—and they were also entitled to presents at weddings and at other important festivals. The tanners, in addition to their share in the harvest, also received as their perquisite hides of dead animals. The services of goldsmiths, potters, tailors, oilmen and dyers, being of a different character, in that they were not directly connected with the daily domestic or farm life, were paid for in cash whenever required, and thus they were considered as independent artisans.

This system of paying for services in kind is gradually being broken down by modern economic conditions. For instance, on account of the great demand for hides, and because of the ready money they bring, the people sell them to the hide-merchants. Leather goods, shoes, etc., being now available anywhere, the services of the tanners can be easily dispensed with. This has thrown thousands of tanners out of work.

Spinning was carried on in almost every family; and whenever people had sufficient yarn they would take it to the village weaver to have it make into cloth. The weaver, of course, received his payment in kind at harvest time; but he was also entitled to a portion of the yarn for his labour. On account of the cheap, machine-made cloth the weaver too has been thrown out of work. In this way almost all the village artisans have suffered on account of the introduction of cheap, machine-made articles imported from outside. Some of these artisans, finding that it was more profitable to be in cities and towns, have migrated there, leaving their villages without their particular trade. Carpenters and blacksmiths, for instance, can make a much better living in towns than they can in villages.

The main object of this department, then, is to revive the local industries and introduce such others as might be profitable to the village people. With this aim in view a careful study of the local industries and their present condition was made in the surrounding villages within a certain area.

**Weaving**

The aims of this section are:

1. To give instruction to a number of apprentices.

2. To teach better designs to the weavers of the locality and to help them by supplying them with raw materials at a price cheaper than they would have to pay if they bought them at the local market, at the same time helping them to market their products. Unless the weavers can be organized into a co-operative group and saved from the clutches of the middlemen, they cannot expect to derive any appreciable profits from their work. Where they have no such co-operative facilities they can hardly make a living. In Bolpur town, which is the nearest place where the weavers of the locality can purchase their yarn, there is only one store that sells the raw materials, and here the poor weavers are at the mercy of the storekeeper. The materials cost them so much that they cannot compete favourably with the machine-made cloth. And if they have to sell their produce at these stores they lose again from the profits of the middlemen.

In addition to the training of apprentices at the Institute, the weaving section is also training a number of women in the villages, chiefly widows, and also supervises the work of those who have received their training at the Institute, but who are still in need of some guidance. Some of the night schools in the villages, organized by the Village Welfare Department, have introduced weaving in their programme of work. This, again, is supervised by this section. The section is under the charge of a trained instructor, who has considerable practical experience. He is assisted by another man whom he trained, and who knows not only his own trade, but understands the spirit of the Institute. The section is equipped with a number of fly-shuttle looms and frames for making carpets, cotton mats and tapes, and also with all the accessories of calico-printing and dyeing.

The courses are very flexible, and are adapted to the needs of individual students according to the amount of time they are prepared to spend at the Institute. They range from three months to two years. Among the apprentices and students who come to this section are young boys from the villages, not necessarily from the weavers' caste. As a matter of fact they come from all castes, from the Brahmin (the highest caste) to the Muchis (one of the lowest castes), with all the other castes between. Then there are teachers deputed from Union and District Board Schools to learn weaving and gardening; also social workers from private organizations.

There are always very heavy demands from outside institutions for the services of the instructor, who is sent out on these missions whenever he can be spared. Many public institutions, such as the "Bani Bhavan," a women's institute founded by Lady Jagadish Chandra Bose, in Calcutta, and the Anatha Ashram (orphanage) in Dacca, have started vocational education in weaving as a result of the training they received from the instructor at Sriniketan. Requests also come from the various district industrial and agricultural exhibitions for a display of our products and for demonstration work.

Allowing for the services that the instructor and his associate devote to the educational work, the section is expected to be on a business footing, and thus show a profit in its working. This is very rigidly insisted upon, for it is only when these different sections are put on such a business basis that we can expect people to take to this industry.

Here it is sufficient to say that as a result of the training given in this section the weavers of the locality have considerably increased their income, others have started weaving as a whole-time industry, yet, in many instances, these people are not weavers by caste. They are all making a very decent living from this trade. Several schools and institutions, not only in the district but also outside, have included weaving in their curriculum, some as a vocational course, others as part of the manual training or industrial arts course.

## Tannery

It is estimated that there are about 3600 Muchis (leather-workers) in the district. A great majority of them are landless, and in most cases have forgotten their own trade. Some of them are farming on small pieces of land on rentals, others earn their living as day-labourers. Their condition is very miserable.

The tannery was started as an experiment, in the face of many difficulties. First of all with regard to the getting of raw materials. All the villages round about, with the exception of two, are Hindu villages; therefore no cows are slaughtered in them for the consumption of flesh. Even in the two Mohammedan villages it is only on the occasion of their annual festivals that they kill cows, and then only a few. The only hides available are from dead carcasses, and from the point of view of tanning these are of very poor quality. It was possible to get hides of good quality from Calcutta, but then the cost of production would have been too heavy; moreover, it would not have been doing any service to the Muchis, for whom it was primarily started. Another difficulty presented itself in the tanning of these hides, the choice of process—bark-tanning or chrome-tanning. More than 90 per cent, of the leather sold in the markets is chrome-tanned—the bark-tanned leathers being required only for suitcase-making, for which the demand is not so great.

During the period that the tannery was working—1924 to 1930—a number of Muchis were trained in their own trade. They are all better off now than they had ever been before. But the purely educational side of the tannery did not seem to be justified, and so it was closed in 1931. It was found, however, that it would be profitable for the Institute, as well as for the Muchis, to manufacture fancy articles of leather, such as hand-bags, embroidered cushion-covers, leather stools (filled with straw), portfolios, etc. So far there has been no difficulty in marketing these articles, and the progress made has been very encouraging to a continuance of this work.

### Carpentry

From 1921 to 1928 the carpentry section, although very poorly housed, was under the direction of an expert Japanese carpenter. But during his severe illness, which resulted in his death in 1928, it was closed. Later on another Japanese took charge of the work, but he gave only half of his time to the training of apprentices.

According to the Bengal Census Report of 1901 carpenters were classed with those artisans who are rapidly decreasing in numbers. Although the wooden plough with its little blade of iron is still in vogue, other agricultural machinery, such as the sugarcane-crushing machine, has been replaced by the improved machine made of iron. The conservative village carpenters would not make anything which they had not been making for generations. There is a growing demand, however, for better furniture and fittings even in the village houses. All these jobs are taken up by the up-country carpenters residing in the towns. If only the village carpenters would take to making new things their trade would be a prosperous one. A number of village carpenters were approached on the subject of sending their boys to the Institute to learn cabinet-making, but they would not avail themselves of the opportunity.

Due to lack of proper housing arrangements and insufficient time at the disposal of the instructor (the Japanese who was also in charge of the vegetable garden) the work of this section did not accomplish much towards the training of apprentices. Since then better accommodation has been secured for this section, and there are enormous possibilities for young men, not only from villages but also from towns, to take up this trade and to earn more than in most of the other professions. There is a great demand for skilled carpenters throughout the entire district, and sometimes it is very difficult to get the services of these people. It is a good chance for the young men of the district to take advantage of the opportunity.

### Lacquer Industry

During the time of the East India Company the lacquer industry in the district was in a very flourishing condition. Ilambazar, a small town about nine miles from Sriniketan, was noted for its lacquer-work. As late as fifty years ago there were approximately sixty families in this town engaged in this work. Now only fourteen are left, and these are in a very poor condition. Most of them are suffering from enlargement of the spleen, kala-azar, and other complications accompanying malaria; and if they are not taken care of they will all disappear, one by one. Two of these families have been persuaded to come to work at Sriniketan. Under the guidance and direction of the artists at the Institute they are now turning out articles of real artistic value, attracting the attention of the art-loving public and creating a demand for such things.

### Pottery

In India the makers of pottery still use old, primitive methods, and the potter's wheel is still a reality. On account of the extreme poverty of the masses the only household utensils for cooking and drinking and eating are earthen post. Some of the people are so poor that they cannot buy even these earthen pots. The result is that even the potters are not able to support themselves by this trade alone, and often have to seek work elsewhere. No effort has been made to improve this industry, although large quantities of china goods are imported into the country from Japan and Europe.

In the whole country there are perhaps not more than half-a-dozen small factories which are producing china wares—or rather modifications of china goods.

In the whole locality there is only one potter, and he too often finds himself out of work. A small plant on modern lines has been set up as an experiment. Nothing can be said about its success yet; but pottery is a craft which can be improved along modern lines.

**Bookbinding, Embroidery and Tailoring**

Art has not yet been commercially utilized as it has been in Europe and America. The old craftsmen are not producing anything new. All their designs are old, and the creative spirit seems to have become deadened. The artists have a great contribution to make to the old arts and crafts of the country. The old arts and crafts of the villages have not only to be revived, but also to be renewed in the light of new experiences and new art. Art is not a static thing. It is living; and Sriniketan is always attempting to improve and introduce the artistic side of village life. The peasant art, however crude, his its place. It is the very soul of the village life. Artistic bookbinding, embroidery and needlework are some of the crafts which can be taken up by village people, not only as hobbies, but also as subsidiary industries.

Tailoring is another trade which has been found to be very profitable in the villages, and yet, there are no tailors to do the work. Coats, shirts, children's and women's garments, ready-made, are sold in towns, and people buy them at the weekly markets. The village people have no idea how much cheaper these articles would be if they were made at home. If only the women knew how to cut out and sew! The widows especially could learn tailoring and could execute orders for their village. In one of the neighbouring villages a widow who had learned a little tailoring at the Institute invested all the money she had in a sewing-machine, and now she is earning a very good living by making garments for only a few families.

There are still a number of cottage industries which can very profitably be introduced in the villages, and the Institute is always on the alert to discover any such industry, along with the right person to direct it.

**Mechanical Workshop**

Machines of all descriptions are daily making their appearance even in the villages. American Fords and Chevrolet cars and buses can be seen tearing down the country roads, connecting villages not yet reached by railways, and carrying loads of passengers of all castes and creeds. The drivers of these cars and buses, although most of them have never had any training as mechanics, are quite capable of handling these machines. There is a great demand for trained mechanics and electricians to make the petty repairs on these cars. Rice mills are to be found throughout the country districts, and are on the increase. Their machinery also needs repair now and then. Even in the field of agriculture the old hand-made tools and implements are gradually being replaced by machine-made ones. A closer examination would reveal the fact that the machine has invaded even the remotest parts of rural India, but the ability to use and to care for machines has lagged.

Modern science and the machine age have reduced drudgery and sweating to its minimum, even for animals, in Western countries; but the Indian farmer and the artisan are still compelled to spend their maximum physical energy in order to obtain the minimum of results. Even the improved type of simple agricultural implements, such as shovels and pickaxes, are beyond their reach.

In Western countries, with the advent of industrialism and the machine age, the blacksmith readily adjusted himself to the changed conditions. In India, however, although large industries are still in their infancy, machines have reached everywhere, and there is a great need for improved agricultural and other implements, which can be manufactured in India in local shops at a much lower cost than they can be imported.

Through the small mechanical workshop and power-house, therefore, it is planned to manufacture simple and improved agricultural implements, and to give practical training to young men in the making of these implements, and in repair work of all kinds, to meet the growing needs of the villagers.

Electricity and all the blessings which the modern machine age has to give are fast coming into the towns and cities. Electric street-cars, automobiles, electric lights, electric pumps, etc., are being introduced into all the cities. The villages must not lag behind. They too deserve their share of the advantages offered by modern conveniences, and therefore need to learn the use of modern machinery.

## VILLAGE WELFARE DEPARTMENT

### Sanitation and Health

No programme of rural reconstruction can be complete without including in it the work of sanitation and health.

The unsanitary condition of Indian villages and the diseases from which the people are always suffering cannot escape the notice of even the most casual visitor. People appear to be living in a perpetual state of ill-health, because of the unsanitary living conditions, malnutrition and ignorance of the elements of personal hygiene.

It is estimated that more than 5,000,000 people in India annually die of preventable diseases, and that the daily death-roll in Bengal caused by malaria alone is 1000. According to the calculations made by Dr. Bentley, Director of the Public Health Department, Bengal, there are on an average 28,300,000 cases of malaria infection in Bengal, out of a total population of 46,500,000. Cholera is another disease which appears almost every year in epidemic form and sweeps away millions of people from the country as a whole. These and many other diseases carry away millions of people prematurely to their graves, and prepare millions to follow.

The poverty-stricken condition of the villages is due in large part to these diseases and epidemics. The people have lost their vitality, their working capacity has greatly diminished, and their economic condition has reached the very bottom. It is an acknowledged fact that public health and economic conditions act and react on each other.

> . . . Disease causes poverty, and poverty causes disease. More than five million of people suffer the death penalty every year from preventable diseases. Many days of work are lost yearly by each worker from the same cause, and the average efficiency of each worker is diminished by about 20 to 30 per cent, from the combined effects of disease and malnutritions.[5]

What far-reaching effects there will be if the health of the people can be improved it is not possible to estimate. By means of improved health the country will be able to utilize the services of all classes of people much more effectively than it can under existing conditions. There would be a decided increase in the production of wealth. How much larger would be the harvest if the cultivator enjoyed good health! His poor physique and days of illness, especially during the cultivation and harvest periods, prevent his getting the maximum return from his land. The economic condition, and with it the whole outlook of the people, can be improved if the living conditions are made more sanitary and if more attention is paid to the promotion of good health.

Perhaps on account of the old idea of solidarity and self-protection, villages in India are very compact, with narrow lanes, and very little space is allowed between the houses. The construction of the dwelling-houses, also, on account of social customs, does not allow for sufficient light and ventilation. Although there is always a courtyard attached to the women's apartments, the women, being busy most of the day in the kitchens, are not able to take advantage of the light and fresh air as much as they should. There is no place set apart for refuse, and each family throws all kinds of refuse and rubbish on the nearest spot. As a result there are heaps of refuse to be found everywhere in the village. The lanes and streets are full of filth. During the rains the lanes are flooded with filth and dirt, the refuse dumps become breeding places of flies, while the pits at the back of the houses become breeding places for mosquitoes. Lt.-Col. Dunn, another authority on public health in India, asserts that "If the laws of health were regarded in India to the same extent as in England, and the same proportion of money was spent on public health, the death-rate in India would be no larger than in England." He goes further, and says that "money spent in training midwives, health visitors and dais under the supervision of medical officers of health in towns would undoubtedly reduce by half the existing death-rate of infants."[6]

Whether or not the laws of health are followed depends largely on the education of the people. Unless they are given an education which will free them from old superstitious habits they cannot be expected to obey these laws, or even understand them. In order to make them a part of their lives the people must understand what these laws are, and why they should be followed. Therefore it is necessary that these people should be educated to the point where they understand the simple rules of health and sanitation.

Experience has proved that when people are shown why they suffer from preventable diseases they become eager to follow such advice, so far as it lies in their power and within their means to do so.

So far as finances are concerned, the District Boards are the only agencies for looking after the health of the rural areas; but, on account of their meagre sources of income, it has not been possible for them to finance an extensive programme of sanitation in the villages. They can hardly support a few dispensaries, which are very poorly equipped. It is necessary for the Provincial and Central governments to participate fully in the sanitary and health programme of the rural areas, although in the long run the success and permanency of the work of sanitation and health will depend entirely upon local initiative and interest. The only way to ensure such a lasting effect is to educate the people, and to organize them into co-operative health societies. The Central Co-operative Anti-Malaria Society, founded by Rai Bahadur Dr. Gopal Chandra Chatterjee, under his able and untiring leadership is doing very valuable work. "Co-operation" is the slogan of the present age, and it is in co-operation that the hope of the villages for their health and sanitation lies. The co-operation of the Government and of the District Boards is certainly essential, for without their aid the poor village societies cannot do very much; and yet it is the co-operation of the village people among themselves that is most necessary. It is only when they have learned the full significance of co-operation, and have discarded the old individualistic ideas, that we can hope for a revival of life in the villages. The upper-class people can no longer make such societies exclusive for themselves. No society can be called co-operative, nor can it function satisfactorily, unless and until it extends its membership to all the inhabitants of the village on an equal footing, and with equal rights and privileges, irrespective of their castes or social status.

The Village Welfare Department of the Institute has under its charge the programme of health and sanitation in the surrounding villages. For this purpose it is equipped with a well-qualified medical staff. There is also a well-equipped dispensary located at the Institute, which takes in out-patients every morning, the afternoons being left for visits to the villages. According to the report of the Institute for 1929, 6760 patients were treated at this dispensary, and their number is on the increase every year.

The same department, with the help of the medical staff, organizes co-operative health societies in the villages within a radius of approximately ten miles, and in some instances at even greater distances. The dispensary is not run on a purely charitable basis. No charge is made for the services of the physician, but the patients are charged the actual cost of the medicines. Those who are members of health societies in their villages get these medicines at a somewhat lower rate, while non-members have to pay the actual cost. In this way people are encouraged to become members of their village co-operative health society. The poor and destitute, however, are given free treatment and free medicines, and in some cases are even provided with food, clothing and shelter. When necessary, the medical staff pays calls. Here again the members are given concessions, while the non-members have to pay the ordinary fee. In all matters pertaining to the question of health and sanitation the medical officer is the supreme authority, and on his advice the department arranges the health programme in the villages. Other workers are sent out to give lantern lectures on malaria and other preventable diseases, and how to combat them. The village Scouts, under the direction of the same department, carry out the programme of anti-malaria work, fire-drills, and checking the spread of epidemics.

The Institute's midwife, who is also a teacher, and good at sewing and embroidery, not only attends maternity cases, but organizes women's societies in the villages, and gives talks on maternity, nursing and the care of the children. She also invites the local village dais (midwives) to the maternity cases, and demonstrates the work to them and to other women of the villages.

It will not be possible for a long time for every village to have midwives trained in hospitals and medical colleges, although every village, through its co-operative societies, can send a woman to receive such a training in a recognized institution. Another way to train the village dais is for each district to have one or two centres where, through the co-operation of the District Boards, the Public Health Department and the co-operative societies, arrangements could be made to offer short courses to these village dais. They might also be supplied with a small outfit to be used in delivery cases.

There is a great dearth of women doctors in India. The few women that are following the profession of medicine are found mostly in cities and towns. The rural areas are totally married and fathered a son all under the affectionate care and at the expense of his elder brother. As a man of conscience he has tried his skill at all the trades available in the village: agriculture, teaching, bank, law court but without success. His elder brother or any one else has not asked or taunted him over his failure to flourish. He would get his daily bread and clothing even if he did not do anything. He is, however, faced with a challenge of life that should he not prove his worth and establish himself independent of any support! When he takes his first step outside his door he stumbles but rises on to next step immediately by busying himself at the studio. The mercurial nature of this venture soon reveals itself and he is again thrown out of gear. He swims back to his tested waters after reflecting that the trade did not let him down, only he could not measure up to its demands. He is a cool headed, dispassionate actor in the scheme of things. Hence he never wails on his failures. Nor does he put the blame at the doors of others. He introspects and guides himself rather than be guided by anyone else. He has a positive attitude to life and everybody around. This attitude generates goodwill for him. Even those who see fault in his good actions as is done by Ravi's father, do not invite his retort. He feels more resolved to continue in his mission because he has developed a perspective that originates in the totality of background circumstances and not in short, impulsive temperament.

He is not attracted towards any vice. Nor does he covet. It never occurs to him that he should have more than the minimum. Amidst the worst display of lechery and avarice, he does not pause. There can be no better model of Gandhian doctrine of social trusteeship. The episode of the old landlord not spending anything on himself, denying the basic needs like a water-tap to tenants, repair and ventilation to their respective portions and the general recognition by all his successor sons, daughters and sons-in-law of this fact is a fine example of how social harmony can be achieved if we realized that we were mere trustees of social wealth and that we must be guided by the consideration oi greater good of greater numbers.

At the film studio Shanti and VGL get thousands, De Mello gets only a thousand for being the most efficient manager of men and material. Srinivas gets only one hundred and fifty for intellectual work. Yet he is happy. Sampath lives in penury with his ill-clad and famished children in an outhouse in a posh locality. Now he is obsessed with procuring lakhs and leading a life of luxuries and sensuousness without ever caring for the direction in which he is headed. He is basically a hard worker, helpful to one and all. He does not hesitate to do errands and mental jobs like lifting the packets on his shoulders at the station, composing matter and operating the printing machine, distributing pamphlets of *The Banner* and then "doing various errands for the studio." (p. 125). He arranges finance for the film, promises to persuade Ravi to marry the granddaughter of the landlord, persuades Somu to withdraw his criminal complaint against Ravi and keeps him at his home without scheming to exploit any of these situations for his personal gratification. He introspects. "What am I in this scheme of things?" (p. 125) but gets and needs no answer because that would be against the concept of a common Indian who exists for existence's sake and tries to be a true servant of humanity.

In this novel Narayan has tried to put various notions devoid of their tinge and complication. The camera in the film studios is propitiated as any Hindu would do a god, although it belongs to De Mello, seemingly a Christian name. But the latter accepts the ash and vermillion on his forehead without grumbling because it alone would bring them profits and may ruin them with losses too, if it were 'sore'. Through this simple incident in a comic vein Narayan sheds light on the timidness of the common man, particularly in business, which is an enterprise solely based on risks. If the possibility of harm can be avoided by indulging a superstition that does not demand effort, expense or adventure, then it is wise on the part of helpless man to ward it off by an ostrich approach. As if life was cosy and secure so that calamities could be solicited! The man of self-confidence does not indulge in small bickerings when he knows that the stakes are higher. It is wiser to conserve energies. Narayan does exactly this because he has to show the disastrous consequences of the misuse of camera—a mechanical device that records physical impression and adds dimensions to human action. Ravi's suppressed desires are roused after he sees Shanti in transparent costume flood-lit from down below. It seems to warn as to the grave consequences of irresponsible and cheap imageries imprinted on the celluloid for exhibition in mesmerizing conditions of Dark enclosures in the nooks and corners of the country. If self-disciplined great scholar Vishwamitra could not resist the charms of heavenly dancer Urvashi, how can we expect ordinary youth to withstand its lure. However, Srinivas is capable of seeing reason and is not swayed. He looks after Ravi with greater sympathy after this incident and decides to keep away from the fountain-head of vice, Sampath. He has passed through so many phases that nothing lures him now. He knows that "Even madness passes. Only existence asserts itself." (p. 209) This is an important message of Narayan counselling patience that is panacea for all ills only if panick could be avoided. Dispassionate view of life is, therefore, an imperative need for true happiness. This is the essence of Gandhism, which is the prime need of turbulent times.

Narayan cannot write without introducing the element of comic in his narratives. In Mr. sampath too there is lots of comic laughter and amusement that springs up at every step and out of ordinary situations. Mr. Sampath is also the most comprehensive attempt of Narayan. It discusses many sundry aspects of life that remained neglected so far. Its protagonist is the editor of a newspaper that has been started out of sincere desire to serve the nation—"national duty" (p. 45). A journalist should never be biased, prejudiced or interested in anything except faithful objective reporting with fear or favour. For the purpose there is a column 'Open Window' that "advocates abolition of slums, congestion and opposes landlords constructing pigsties for humans." (p. 6). This can be done not by condemning the acts and actors but by juxtaposing the constant war that goes on between man's inside and outside. It is desirable that the positive side of man is supported, strengthened and protected in every possible manner without giving away the feeling or impression of outside interference. Malgudi, like the rest of India, must also witness changes in material, physical, social and moral fabric. Three-four cotton mills have opened indicating its industrialisation. This has opened up opportunities for employment and poor people have started flocking to this city of new hope and promise of betterment to the deprived and the dispossessed. This influx from the neighbouring districts has, however, created problems of housing, sanitation, cooking food in the open and sleeping on pavements. Roads and water-storage tanks are being built on a fast pace. Malgudi is no longer an ordinary town but a fast developing city where film-making facilities are available. North and Western Indians are a common sight in this city of South India and there are no social, racial or regional tensions. All these people are at ease and busy contributing to and enriching the life here. Economic opportunity and the consequent prosperity is awaiting. This scenario also gives away the impression of Gandhi's drem India in the making at Malgudi.

# 'The Financial Expert'

*The Financial Expert* (1995) deals with the rapid rise and fall of Margayya. He is a descendent of corpse bearers whose later generations acquired land and came to be known as agriculturists. He lives in a hut near the dreaded and desolated cremation ground. His father left him no property and no cash worth the name. He is married and has a son Balu. To make a living with the help of little education that he has, he sits under a tree, in yellowed shirt and dhoti, with an old tin box and a torn and reickety umbrella. His box contains forms of application for loan, usurped from the Central Cooperative Land Mortgage Bank of Malgudi. He helps illiterate and ignorant peasants from the countryside to seek loan by filling forms for them and keeping a parallel account of their debts and balances with the Bank. If someone does not need a loan, he induces him to seek it still and lend that money to someone who needs it although not eligible to apply for it. In the process he earns his commission and interest on his own small landings. But he runs into trouble after his spoilt son Balu one day throws away his accounts book into the gutter. He quarrels with the peon of the Bank and invites the wrath of the Secretary of the Bank. Consequently he is insulted and dislodged from his place.

Margayya takes this insult seriously and attributes it to his dirty appearance. He visits the priest of the temple who advises him to seek the benevolence of Goddess Lakshmi. He prescribes a ritual in which Margayya is to do puja for forty days with a red lotus burned and mixed with the ghee of a smoke coloured cow. But the goddess's blessings in the form of wealth do not descend on him even after many days of the faithful conclusion of the puja. He faithfully observes all the precautions and fulfills all that is needed as prescribed by the priest. As advised, he goes to look for red lotus in the pond outside the city near a ruined temple. There he meets Dr. Pal, who claims to be a journalist and a sociologist, having sought refuge in the ruins of the temple because it is a place removed away from all the disturbances and noise. Finding Margayya in a desolate place like that and hesitant to enter the deep waters of the pond and yet desirous of a red lotus, he volunteers to pluck one for him. Margayya sees him going on his bicycle one day while he had come out of his house after many days of completion of the puja and fruitless wait for the showers of wealth as a consequence thereof. Dr. Pal takes him to his office and shows him the manuscript of his book 'Bed Life or Domestic Harmony', and tells him of the excellent prospects of earning a lakh of rupees easily. As a friendly gesture he offers it to Margayya in exchange for the contents of his purse—twenty five rupees.

Margayya takes it to one Lal for printing. After much tough bargaining, he enters into an agreement with Lal as equal partners in the venture. The book sells like hot cake and money starts rolling in. After sometime, when the sales fall, he decides to opt out of the partnership and sells his rights to Lal. He opens an account with the Town Bank with the fat amount he has received in the bargains and starts the business of lending money to villagers. Meanwhile there is War boom and he realises that people have acquired lots of money by corrupt means, profiteering and black-marketing. He seeks the help of Pal in soliciting deposits from such people since Pal has very wide contacts. The news of Margayya offering such as high rate of interest on deposits, spreads. At the beginning people are sceptical but their trust is strengthened by the news of prompt payment of interest or deposit on time. There is a huge rush of depositors. Money piles up in bags and has to be transported home and every available space in his house is occupied by bundles of notes. Margayya does not get time even to eat food or to have a talk with his wife.

Balu has always been a problem with him. He is not interested in studies. With the rise in the fortunes of Margayya, his anxiety for his son rises too. With the sole aim of seeing his son to rise high so that he could be sent abroad, he manages to become the Secretary of his son's school. The Head Master and all the teachers become respectful to him. They ignore Balu's faults and tolerate his mischiefs. Margayya even appoints a teacher Murty to give Balu tuitions. The performance of Balu in the examinations is, however, miserable and all the rebukes and persuasions of his father yield no results. Balu fails miserably and tears off the S.S.L.C. register from his school; throws it off into the Malgudi gutter and runs away from home declaring that studies are beyond his capacity. He goes to Madras and becomes a supervisor of sand-wich boys of a cinema theatre, Central Talkies, owned by a mad philosopher. This madman is in the habit of keeping the run-away boys engaged gainfully while at the same time informing the parents, of the death of the boy. Margayya, however, does not feel moved after receiving the letter of the death of Balu, to the consternation of all the relatives. But, ultimately, he is compelled to proceed to Madras and with the help of a kind and sincere Police inspector, finds out Balu. Balu, however, is reluctant but the inspector and the philosopher force him to go with his father. In order to prevent recurrence of such an event, Margayya asks Balu to eat, rest and have as much money as he needs and never touch the book. He also sends Sastri, his accounts-clerk to look for a suitable match. The daughter of a landowner of Mempi Hills is finally selected and even though their horoscopes don't match, an astrologer is found by Pal who declares that they match. The marriage takes place and Balu is given a separate house to live in amidst all the comforts secured. He, however, has been encouraged to live in luxuries and has acquired vices of wining-womanising in the company of Pal. Margayya suspects the bad influence of Pal on his son in his increasing demands for money. One day Balu comes to demand his share in the wealth of his father. Margayya becomes upset and slaps him. He also decides to find out the truth of the rumours of wining-womanising by Balu. He visits his son's place one night and is told by Balu's wife Brinda of very late arrivals and revelries of Balu with Pal as his constant companion. Margayya decides to remove Pal from the company of his son slowly and tactfully. But while coming out of Balu's house, he finds the car entering with the merry voices of girls. Pal is also in the car. Margayya loses control and beats Pal with his sandle. Pal reports the matter to the police and the next morning goes to tell everybody that money in the hands of Margayya is not safe. Soon people start gathering outside his house demanding back their deposits. The more Margayya gives away, the more the crowd swells. Soon, all the money is exhausted but the restless crowd continues to grow. Ultimately he sends his brother a message across the wall to send for the police and the lawyer. He declares himself bankrupt and surrenders all that he has to save his life. The only thing left to him at the end is his original tin box. He suggests to his son to make a beginning with the contents of the box. Balu has no courage to accept this advice. So, Margayya decides to make a fresh beginning himself. He tells his son, "Very well then, if you are not going, I am going on with it, as soon as I am able to leave this bed."

*The Financial Expert* is based on an actual incident known to Narayan. There existed an 'original of Margayya whose rates of interest lured princes and professors, scientists and civil servants and who made fool of them all.' Narayan has recreated the incident with implications marvellously unfolded. The story moves on two planes: the physical as well as on mystical and at both the planes its structure is superb. On the physical plane it depicts the life in the towns of south India with their local hustle and bustle: their isolated quarrels and tribulations; their social relationships and conduct. Margayya is a common lower middle class man who always burns with a desire to have a chance with luck while still busy tackling the problems of day-to-day existence. His rise is not phenomenal. His great grand fathers began- as corpse bearers; their progeny as small landholder. They could never have more than sufficient to meet their minimum needs. Margayya, therefore, does not inherit more than a rupee, some junk and a half of a small house near the cremation ground. These are not extraordinary circumstances. His vocational beginning, however, is different from those of his parents and grandparents: They were workers and depended on their two hands for livelihood. Margayya is atonce different in that he wields pen instead of working farm-tools. He deals in cash in stead of crops and that too belonging to others. Thus, *The Financial Expert* seeks to eulogise the rewards of pen in preference over those of the yoke. By showing Margayya without educational qualifications, it is Narayan's intention to demonstrate the superiority of intelligence over mere academics. Dr. Pal weilds the pen and knows the worth of his writings too. Yet, he wanders in search of paupers like Margayya and is content with a mere twentyfive in preference over entrepreneurship promising lakhs. Thus, almost all the situations and personage and juxtapositions are highly ironical. In contrast with Margayya who strives hard to rise from abject dust to the heights of the glories of wealth, there is his son Balu who has no inclination to earn at all. He inherits the traits of his father to be a master rather than be a subject. He wants to make an humble beginning as the supervisor of sand-wich boys and is quite happy at his situation. Margayya, on the other hand is never happy. Even though he has millions he does not intend to enjoy, Balu enjoys the fruits of the toil of his father. Margayya is perhaps the greatest yogi who believes in karma with sincerity and devotion without being swayed by the lure of its fruit. He does not indulge the luxuries of any kind even though he becomes the master of millions because he considers this wealth not his but only a trust with him. He has to hand it over to their rightful claimants as and when they demand and, that's what he does when the time comes. He does not weep or suffer from the loss of wealth and is ready to begin again. He is really a victor over Maya.

The excellence of *The Financial Expert* can be better appreciated at the mystical level. Margayya has no initials to indicate his place of origin. He is a descendant of corpse-bearers. His abode is near the cremation ground. The cremation ground is the place where the ashes remain after the corpse is consumed by fire. All the faiths and philosophies acknowledge physical being as the product of the soil to which it goes back ultimately. Naturally, therefore, the next stage in the family of cropse-bearers is that of land-tillers and the next that of holders of small tracts of land. No one wants to own the dead. But the ashes of the dead mixed with the soil make it fertile for a fresh crop. What is mortal is earthly. The unearthly is the soul that leaves for higher regions to merge with the parmatman—the One Supreme. The mortal imprisons the immortal and the seeming co-existence of the two is the result of the illusion—Maya. Narayan spreads a sort of maya-jal in the name of *The Financial Expert* by indulging the game of a fantastic mislead. He says that 'marga' meant 'the way', and 'ayya' was an honorific suffix. But when joined, the two become Margayya that also means, Sanskritwise, 'the mirge', which befits the story as a whole better than the explanation offered in the story itself. Because the pursuit of wealth in which Margayya is involved is in fact a pursuit of maya—illusion; and his name means the pursuer of illusion, too.

This is amply authenticated by the text of *The Financial Expert*. Lakshmi, the goddess of wealth in Hindu mythology, rides an owl—a bird that preys only in the night. The owl is a bad omen otherwise. It lives in desolated places. Margayya's determination to devote himself to the worship of Lakshmi, immediately brings him in contact with Her messenger Pal, living in the ruins of a temple. Pal volunteers to fetch the red lotus by invading the deep, marshy waters of the pond. This symbolises benevolent approval by Lakshmi of Margayya's desire to seek Her as a devotee. As soon as, therefore, Margayya emerges from the confines of his home after the completion of forty days of devoted worship, Pal meets Margayya again and rather coerces him to accept the treasure-map in the dubious looking form of *Domestic Harmony*. Margayya pounces upon the book and its sales bring him lots of money. But, Margayya's hunger is not satisfied. So, Pal is directed to appear again and help him get located strategically. When the goddess finds Margayya still not happy, she sends the messenger again—this time to open the floodgates of wealth directly since Margayya demonstrated his sincerity of devotion to Her. Soon after rolling in the floods of wealth, however, he loses control over his faculties and commits the most heineous crime of beating the messenger of the goddess itself. By over beating him with his shoes Margayya is guilty of overtraffiking the only bridge between him and his chosen destiny. The bridge breaks in the darkness of night and Margayya is thrown into the gurgling waters. He is swept and washed to the shore alive, however, because of chief virtue that amidst the uncountable wealth he keeps himself untempted to squander or to misappropriate. He does not hesitate part with it. The most impressive and redeeming feature of the story is that Margayya is unrepentant and still a master of himself even after rolling down the heights of glories to the depths of originality. This is because he is an untiring pursuer of Maya that has no end. This is how alone the cycle can go on.

# 'Waiting for the Mahatma'

In *Waiting for the Mahatma* (1955) Sriram, a twenty year old parentless boy, lives with his grand mother at his two hundred year old ancestral house, No. 14 in Kabir Street, at the legendary town of Malgudi. His father had died fighting for the British in Mesopotamia. Every month, therefore, the postman brings a money-order of his family pension which his granny deposits with the Bank next door, known as Fund Office. At his twentieth birthday, she takes Sriram to the Fund Office and finally hands over the account to be solely operated by him henceforth. Sriram is bewildered to find himself the master of thirty eight thousand five hundred rupees, seven annas and six pice and fills up a withdrawal form for the maximum permissible amount of two hundred fifty rupees at a time, to test his newfound authority. He is persuaded, however, to withdraw fifty. As soon as he comes out, he buys four anna worth of coloured drinks and bananas at Kanni's shop opposite his house. Kanni had been a supplier of cheroots to his grand father who had left a debt of nine rupees twelve annas, which is now realised square off to the a mount of ten rupees in a note handed over by Sriram. He also buys a canvas chair for seven rupees for his grandmother, but she spurns it because it is made of leather. Since he belongs to a traditionally propertied household, Sriram is required to do nothing except to eat and while away the time for the next four years. One day in April, he is approached on the road by a beautiful girl with a collection-box. Sriram is dumb before her and drops an eight-anna coin in the box which, he is told by the jaggery merchant, is being collected for the visit of Mahatma Gandhi. A huge crowd gathers on the banks of Saryu to listen to the Mahatma. Sriram goes there in search of the girl whom he finds sitting near the Mahatma. He too manages to sit in the first row. The Mahatma, after speaking of truth and non-violence, goes to stay in a hut in the sweepers' colony along the Saryu. Sriram too goes and sits near him in the hut until Gandhi retires for the night. He introduces himself to Bharati whose father died in the 1920 movement and mother soon thereafter. She asks Sriram to be truthful and non-violent if he wanted to be nearer Gandhiji. She asks him to come at 3 in the morning to be introduced to the Mahatma. The Mahatma asks him to observe truth and non-violence and stay with him. He also asks Sriram to learn to operate the Spinning Wheel and wear cloth made by the self only. Going to jail and abstaining from all the comforts of life is imperative for the followers of Gandhi and Sriram agrees to do all that is expected of him by Bharati. The Mahatma also asks Sriram to seek the permission of his granny before joining him.

Sriram joins Gandhi's entourage and walks from village to village in company with Bharati and Gorpad. Bharati is an adopted daughter of Gandhiji and is appointed incharge of Sriram before Bapu leaves by train. Now he lives in a deserted temple in the forests of Mempi. When he spins enough yarn, Bharati sends it to Madras and receives, in exchange, cloth for a dhoti and a jibba but the chappals have not arrived from Wardha. So, Sriram goes without footwear. Since it is a lonely place, he is overcome with desires. Bharati does not encourage him although she does not hesitate to admit that she too is inclined towards him. She cannot do anything without the approval of Bapu, which she promises to seek. She brings him the message of work in that area and leaves to visit again. Sriram writes 'Quit India' all over the area and encounters many of his countrymen afraid of kicking a row with the government and losing their incomes. An English estate Manager Mathieson tells him that he too belongs to India and would not quit and is not afraid of nationalists. He realises that the countrymen loyal to the government temper with his writings and jeer at him at public places. So, he decides to seek instructions from the Mahatma. Meanwhile Bharati comes with the message that they should be guided by their inner voice and faith and not by visuals. Since it is a lonely place, Sriram falls upon her and urges her to marry him there and then. But, Bharati excuses herself unless permitted by Gandhiji, although she does not resist his touch and embrace. She leaves him to come back soon with the message that they may surface now and court arrest. Sriram does not agree and remains there while Bharati goes back and courts arrest and is lodged in the Old Slaughter House.

One day a stranger named Jagdish comes and tells Sriram that he too is a national worker of the order only slightly different from Gandhi. He plants a secret two-way radio behind the idol in the temple. He brings newspapers and other literature inciting people and the army to revolt. He easily dominates Sriram to get many things done, like sticking of secret message-bills and their distribution among armymen.

# 'The Guide'

*The Guide* (1958) is the story of Raju. He is the son of a vendor at the railway station of Malgudi. Much before the arrival of the railways however, his father had built up the house at a desolated site opposite the present station, with his own hands. The arrival of the railways brings prosperity to him and opens up Malgudi for tourist traffic. Scores of people come to see the ancient caves in the Mempi forests which have antique paintings of great cultural importance. Raju is automatically introduced to this trade because he had to sit on the shop of his father at the platform. He knows Tamil and has studied at the Board High School for some time. He is famous as Railway Raju and visitors ask for him the first thing at the Malgudi station. His friend Gaffur operates a taxi and stands by the fountain at the market square.

Once a scholar of ancient culture, Marco comes to visit Malgudi to study the paintings in the caves. Raju lodges him at the Anand Bhavan Hotel and takes him to show the caves in Gaffur's taxi. Soon, thereafter, Marco's wife Rosie comes too. She has an M.A., "not very glamorous...but she did have a figure, slight and slender one, beautifully fashioned, eyes that sparkled, a complexion, not white but dusky." She comes of a temple dancers' family. Marco married her after advertising for a bride with education and good looks. She is. however, not interested in Marco's passion for paintings and objects of art. Rising with good temperament but sleeping after quarrel is their routine. On such an occasion betraying his relationship with his wife, Marco affords an opportunity to Raju to be closer to Rosie. As a tourist guide, praising and flattering has become Raju's second nature and he succeeds marvellously with Rosie. Dancing is her weakness which is detested by Marco as 'street acrobatics'. But Raju tries his trick by praising her talent for dance to the extent he succeeds in establishing sexual relationship with her after whetting her disaffection for Marco.

All this comes to the notice of Marco very soon and he abandons Rosie at the Malgudi station before leaving for Madras. She comes to stay with Raju in his house and starts practising dancing. These developments become intolerable to his mother and she leaves with her brother for his village. Raju's shop at the platform is swindled too by his assistant and he is indebted to the Sait for eight thousand rupees. The shop is allotted to another contractor. The creditor Sait files criminal case against Raju for assaulting him. But he does not abandon Rosie. After she had enough practice, he secures a chance for her dance performance at the Albert Mission College Students' function. It proves a break-even incident and Rosie becomes a shooting star-dancer. Her name is changed to Nalini and invitations for her performance come from all the corners of south India. Huge amounts are paid in advance and she is always booked. Raju too becomes a respectable person with judges, ministers, officers, mill-owners seeking his company. His household has several servants, a driver and a Gurkha watchman.

One day Raju receives a book *The Cultural History of South India* sent by the publishers of Marco. He does not show or talk about it with Rosie. After some time he finds an insured envelop addressed to Rosie from the lawyers of Marco. It contains a document for the release of a jewellary-box to be signed by Rosie. Fearing revival of feelings for Marco in the heart of Rosie, Raju forges her signatures on the document and sends it back. Soon he is arrested on the complaint of Marco. In spite of the best efforts of Rosie, he is sentenced to two years' imprisonment. While in jail he was a model prisoner and used to be referred to as a teacher. But, after his release, he comes to the village of Mangal and camps at an old desolated temple on the banks of Saryu.

The poor, ignorant but innocent villagers gather faith in him and start flocking round him for solutions to their personal problems. They come to believe that his mere look transforms a person. They bring him offerings of fruit, rice and milk and clothes on festivals. They start calling him the Swami. Many years pass by thus. Then, there is a general failure of rains. Drought results in famine. Food brawls and murders start taking place. In his humility Raju sends a message to one Velan and other villagers to stop quarreling, otherwise he would not eat. The message is sent through an idiot who reports that the Swami informs that he would not eat until it rains. Villagers from far and near start thronging the place to have the glimpse of the holy man who has ventured to fast and pray for rains. Newspapers flash this news and several governmental agencies come to exploit the potential of the congregation there. Raju tries his utmost to explain to Velan that he never intended to fast for rains and does not want to do it. He tells Velan of his past life of crime and lust. But the reverence for his holy appearance with long beard and hair is so stupefying that Velan does not react except with renewed submission. Raju has no option but to rise to the demands of the situation. He undertakes to fast and pray in the knee-deep waters for the arrival of rains. At the eleventh day, he collapses while praying in the river-bed with the prophesy that it has started raining in the hills.

*The Guide* is thus a very powerful story. Like *Financial Expert* and *The Man-Eater of Malgudi, The Guide* too has a strong mythological base.

# 'The Man-Eater of Malgudi'

The story of *The Man-Eater of Malgudi* (1962) is centred on Vasu who calls himself a taxidermist. He has a 'tanned face, large powerful eyes under thick eyebrows, a large forehead and a lock of unkempt hair, like a black buffalo'(17). He visits Natraj, the narrator, at his printing press one day to order printing of five hundred letter heads and an equal number of visiting cards to be delivered the next day. However he returns only after a fortnight. He has studied at Presidency College, Madras and has Master's degrees in History, in Economics and in Literature. He has participated in the Civil Disobedience Movement against the British rule and has been in jail. After his release from the prison, once he found himself in the streets of Nagpur where a pahelwan adopted him and nourished him with a hundred almonds, a seer of milk, six eggs with honey, chicken and rice, vegetables and fruit every day. He made him strong and trained him to be steel fisted so that he could 'snap chains, twist iron bars, and pulverize granite.' (21) When his guru the pahelwan became old, Vasu hit him with the edge of his palm and left him squirming, in reaction against his show of anger and abuse. Thereafter, he went to Junagadh and met Suleiman who was a master at stuffing a lion to make it look more terrifying dead than alive.

Vasu visits Natraj again at a time when the latter is haggling with a junk buyer over the price of the heap of old useless papers lying in the attic of his press. Vasu suggests that he should be allowed to stay in the attic until he could get some vacant bungalow. Since he is new to Malgudi and starts calling Natraj by his first name in the manner of an intimate friend, Natraj finds it impossible to prevent him from occupying the attic. Vasu moves into the premises without bothering to seek Natraj's approval. He has to stay in Malgudi because of Mempi Forest where he goes to hunt tigers, hyenas, bears, eagles and every other creature that catches his eye or he hears about. Once he takes Natraj, for ten minutes, in his jeep and abandons him at the bus stop, disappears on a hunt for a tiger. Natraj has no money and survives on the tea and buns offered by Muthu and, reaches home at eleven in the night only on the recommendation to the bus conductor to charge him the fare after he reaches home. Vasu does not care for rules and permits. When he finds it difficult to hunt in the forest, he starts killing domestic animals like pet dogs and even squirrels.

He tans the skins and stuffs them in the attic itself. Soon the surroundings are full of stench. Neighbours complain to authorities and Natraj finds his own stay in the press unbearable. He gathers courage to ask Vasu to vacate the attic. But Vasu lodges a complaint against his forcible eviction by Natraj, so the Court summons are issued against the latter. Natraj is scared and seeks the services of a lawyer to get the hearing adjourned. Meanwhile, forest officials also get suspicious of poaching in the forest and hunt for Vasu. Vasu, however, accuses Natraj of complaining to the forest officials against him. He declares that he does not care and threatens Muthu, the tea-vendor at the foot hills of Mempi, of dire consequences for having informed the forest officials about his hunts. He also barricades his entrance to the attic and ties a stuffed hyena at the entrance of the staircase itself. Soon, several types of loose women are seen visiting him in the darkness of the night. One of them is Rangi, the temple-dancer. He takes a fancy to her and her cooking.

Natraj has for his intimate friends, a poet and a journalist Sen. Sen's favourite pastime is to criticise the Nehru government's policies and priorities. The poet is busy writing poetry on the immortal love of Lord Krishna and Radha. At the completion of the portion where Krishna is to meet his future beloved Radha, Natraj decides to celebrate this event in the life of his friend, the budding poet. Astrologers are consulted and a day held out to be not so good, is chosen because it coincides with the festival of the temple on a full moon day. Appeals for the collection of funds are made in order to celebrate the occasion of launching the poet into prominence. The municipal committee Chairman, a Congressman and a sweet-vendor by profession, is invited to preside over the function. Kumar, the temple elephant in the care of Muthu would naturally be the star attraction of the procession. Handbills inviting donations are distributed far and wide but Vasu is ignored. However, he manages to get one and bursts upon Natraj and company for ignoring him. He takes out a ten rupee note to donate but on the insistence of Natraj for not less than a hundred rupees from him, he takes away the green folder itself which contains the list of hundred-rupee donors. There is a scare in the town at Vasu on his collection drive. He neither shows the folder nor renders the accounts, when money is demanded of him. He has plans to shoot the temple elephant, moreover, and has already obtained rights on the dead elephant. There is a scare and Natraj informs the police D.S.P. on the basis of information from Rangi and also after talking to Vasu himself. On the visit of the police inspector, Vasu hits him with the back of his hand and throws away his whistle. There is a scare among the witnesses and the police inspector threatens him of the consequences of hitting him on duty. With great efforts of Natraj to save lives and order on the procession day, the route is changed. Vasu, however, is found dead in his chair near the window overlooking the road of procession. There is speculation over the motive for Vasu's death and suspicion rests on the police inspector, then Rangi, then Natraj himself. But the fact is that Vasu killed himself in the process of smashing two mosquitoes on his forehead.

*The Man Eater of Malgudi* is the most comprehensive novel written by Narayan so far. Malgudi is copiously described for the first time with its Market Road, behind which is Kabir Street. There is the New Extension besides Adam's Lane, Vinayak Street and the charming Nelappa's Grove. There is Albert Mission School too. The sweep of action reaches Mempi forests and the life in this region is microscopically examined. The Bus service breaks down and on such break downs its conductor thrives. The police officers connive at such corrupt practices because they themselves exploit the situation. India, fresh after its Independence is a scene of wastage of resources and the talent as evidenced from Dr. Joshi's account of the lack of facilities for the treatment of animals. A little informed people like Sen are happy in criticising and fault-finding with the government. 'Peace and non-violence preached by Gandhi earlier, manifest in the lack of initiative and courage among the people. This state of existence encourages rakshasas like Vasu to thrive.

The novel besides bringing Malgudi's life into close focus, also offers a glimpse of the quiet flow of south-Indian life with its leisures, pleasures and preferences and its anxieties. The temple has its own world and the elephant and a woman dancer are its permanent distinguishing features. In fact, temple in south India offers a platform for social activity too. Small ripples like Vasu in the vast ocean of life cause too much turbulence. They are the product of new times. Highly educated from the big metropolis of Madras, Vasu poses a threat to the simple folk-life of Malgudi. With his superior knowledge, hardened physique and bullying demeanour, he easily assumes demonic proportions. The poor townsmen with their best of knowledge, courage and resources are just infants before him. In calling him a man-eater Narayan has aimed hard at the new breed of persons coming out of institutions of new times. Products of a system based on sentimentalism which provides ample opportunity of education available to one and all for a mere asking, a new class of privilege seekers is mushrooming. With no cultural background and no moral base, Vasu can only bully and ridicule the soft and amiable people like Natraj and the poet. Any show of courtsey to them is interpreted as a sign of weakness, rather spinelessness. Alertness, wit and a readiness to retort and resist hoodwinking alone earn their appreciation. But, the simple and peace-loving people are incapable of such a display. So, their property and freedoms are imperilled. This does not augur well for a newly independent nation.

The structure of the novel is tight and the plot is full of layers of suspense. It is full of humourous situations. The irony is at its best displayed in *The Man-Eater of Malgudi.* It begins with the beginning of the story that tells of the breaking of the traditional joint households due to the petty quarrels and women's jealousies. Vasu plants himself in Natraj's attic; never bothers to say a word about payments; snatches the green-folder containing the list of big donors; files a complaint of harassment of his tenants against Natraj without ever being his tenant or paying him a paisa for rent—these situations are truly ironical. All this is possible because he is always alert and assertive. The much dreaded police inspector finds himself nonplussed when asked if he had a warrant to enter his premises. The inspector collapses at one stroke of Vasu. Narayan, with his heart in the lot of the poor, simple village-folk must be wishing—'only if the common simple folk could be anywhere near a match for Vasu!'

Natraj is an honest hard working and a modest person. As a printer he does his job carefully and very sincerely. He is content with whatever legal income he derives from his printing press. He has regard for the old machine-man who in turn is devoted to his job without complaining against the working conditions. He does his job single-handedly by both composing the matter and by operating machines himself. Natraj himself is an amiable person. He is not covetuous by nature. His well in manneredness is abused by Vasu when he occupies the attic without promising to pay any rent. Not only does he not pay any rent but he constantly exploits Natraj by not paying him for the printing job. When Natraj is sick of the behaviour of Vasu he wants his premises vacated. Vasu goes to the extent of filing a complaint against Natraj for illegally dislodging him from his premises. Natraj's generosity is further demonstrated in his undertaking to publish the poetry of his friend "The Budding Poet" and thus launching him on to a way to fame. Here, monetary transactions are not involved, not to speak of profits. Even in their attempt to collect donations from the public for the temple celebrations, Natraj and company are selfless and a devoted lot. They are not only for the temple and its elephant but also for the general well-being of the people of the town. Compared to this is the miserable attitude of Vasu who is inhuman in his approach and demonic in his dealings with everyone.

As a young desciple he killed his guru and deserted Suleiman Pahelwan too, who taught him the art of stuffing the animals. Nothing can be expected of persons like Vasu. They occupy other's property unauthorisedly and do not pay for the work done by others for them. And on the top of it they would collect charities and donations for a public cause only to misappropriate the whole amount. They can beat the police officers and they can kill the animals whether wild or domestic. Such people are truly demonic compared to the well behaved but poor Sens and Natrajs. Nothing better can be expected of them. The picture of Vasu that emerges after a reading of The Man-Eater of Malgudi is therefore identical with that of the mythical Bhasmasur although on a miniature scale. As Bhasmasur became a danger to the existence of all the right type of people so Vasu becomes a threat to the peaceful existence of the people of Malgudi. As Bhasmasur was destroyed by the very force of his boon, so Vasu is also destroyed by the force of his slap in the process of killing mosquitoes on his forehead. He is an embodiment of extreme brutal physical force which he uses to harrass the simple innocent people of Malgudi. But that very force is ordained to become the source of his undoing.

# 'The Vendor of Sweets'

*The Vendor of Sweets* (1967) is one Jagan who lives at Lawley Extension and has his sweets shop in the market. He is a true follower of Mahatma Gandhi and has been to jail as a satyagrahi. He rises at five in the morning and brushes his teeth with the margosa twig. He spins on the Charkha everyday for an hour and wears a dhoti and jibba made of self-spun yarn. He ensures his footwear are made of naturally dead cow or calf. He abstains from sugar, salt and rice and lives on boiled vegetables and stone-ground wheat, cooked by himself. He could not pass his B.A. in spite of many attempts and joined Gandhi's movement after the latter has come to address a huge gathering on the banks of the river. He has written a book *Nature Cure and Natural Diet* which is due for printing at the Truth Printing for many years. His father started with a thatched hut but built the present house brick by brick after much litigation.

Jagan's son Mali was born ten years after his marriage with Ambika after a pilgrimage to the shrine of Santana Krishna. Ambika, however, died of a rare brain tumour when Mali was ten years old. Jagan, therefore, tolerates everything from Mali with indulgence. One day Mali tells him that he is not interested in studies because he finds it worthless. Then he engages himself in writing a novel. But before he is able to write it, he decides to go to America to learn the art of writing. He steals ten thousand rupees from the secretly hidden unaccounted money. Without the knowledge of his father he goes to Madras to obtain his passport and to buy his air-ticket. When he returns from America he brings Grace whom he keeps as his wife. She is an orphan of a Korean mother and American father. She was employed in America and came to India to marry Mali in Indian style. Mali comes with the scheme of manufacturing 'story-writing machines' in India in collaboration with some American company which will provide the know-how and technical personnel and promotional material. About fifty-one thousand dollar worth of Indian capital would have to be raised by Mali. He wants his father to finance his project. He also plans to raise capital from the public with the support of the cousin of his father who is a regular visitor. Grace starts conducting herself as a devoted Indian daughter-in-law by sweeping floor, washing clothes and vessels and tidying Jagan's room. Jagan is not inclined to finance his son's project which he considers absurd. He starts avoiding contact with his son and Grace, which has been rare in the past, by using the backdoor. Soon Grace goes to live with her friends because she has been rejected by Mali who says he cannot afford to keep her longer.

Jagan realises the futility of earning enormous income by his sweets shop which has resulted in wastage by his son. He had been given kitchen duties while in jail. So he decided to become a vendor of sweets. He has never sold adulterated or substandard stuff even though prices of raw material rise or they become scarce. Everyday small school-children pass by his shop with hungry looks. Now he decides to cut down prices and hangs a placard announcing 'any packet twentyfive paise'. There is a huge crowd and nothing remains unsold within an hour of opening of sales in comparison with several items remaining unsold and hence going waste earlier. A crisis in the market is created and the sait of Anand Bhavan and the government Canteen-contractor together with a white-bearded man call on him in a delegation and urge upon him to desist from ruining their business. The white-bearded man is Chinna Dorai, a sculptor of the images of gods, turned hair-drier. He takes him to show the image of five-faced Gayatri left unfinished by his guru and advises Jagan to buy up the place near the cremation grounds and instal that idol. Jagan feels reminded of the message of Bhagvad Gita to dissociate from worldly objects and interests after a certain age and adopt the ascetic way of living. He decides to renounce the world: Mali, his sweets-shop, everything. He makes his unnamed cousin incharge with the hope sooner or later Mali will come down to the earthy reality and start looking after the business.

# 'Painter of Signs'

The *Painter of Signs* (1967) is one Raman, past thirty, who lives with his aunt Laxmi in Ellaman Street. His parents died in a train accident and the aunt and Raman alone survived. Aunt Laxmi, 75 now, became a widow early after her Head constable husband died leaving her without a child. She looks after Raman as her child and is fully attentive to his dietary needs. She buys all grocery from Chettiar Shop and the rest of the time is spent at the temple where religious discourses take place in the evenings. Several proposals of marriage of Raman have come from respectable families of "officers, judges and rich men" which have been ready to accept and treat him "like a prince" and give "all the comfort" that he may want (p. 153). Only six months ago a proposal came with the offer of a dowry of five thousand. But, Raman has been declining to marry at all. "He had chosen to remain a bachelor, in spite of the several opportunities that came his way to choose a bride for himself." (p. 45)

He is a signboard painter and prefers to call himself a "lettering artist". In this pursuit he runs about on his bicycle doing the work in the backyard of his house on the river bank and delivering the board and also fixing it at the appointed place. This business is full of risks because he rarely gets the contracted amount and more often his customers point out some deficiency in the finished product even if it were according to the specifications dictated by the customer. Raman is, however, content because he keeps a lot of margin between the actual cost of material and the price quoted. He quoted thirty rupees to the lawyer and received ten rupees in advance and nothing after the job was over. The bangle-seller pays him fifty five against seventy five quoted, only because he has to seek Raman's recommendation to the lady in the Family Planning Department. He has also realized that there is great scope for the business because of expanding trade and other economic and professional activities in the town. However, all those who need a new board or an old board repainted, are basically dishonest. It is these people like Gupta who close old business and begin a new one every year by merely changing the board to confound Sales Tax and Income Tax men. Those who are genuine like Chettiar don't need even a repainting of the board because they are known for their business integrity and people would flock to their shops even if the board is not intelligible.

Though Raman has ruled out marriage, he is potent and sex attracts him. Once he sees a woman bathing in the river with her clothes lifted up to her thighs. His eyes waver and wander over to her nakedness. He is introduced by his friend Veerappa, one day, to Daisy at the Family Planning Centre. Daisy wants him to paint a board for her office and later asks him to accompany her on a three week official tour to the countryside for selecting sites for Family Planning messages. Raman finds Daisy very young, very attractive in sari and wonders at her Christian name. No one knows anything abut her: her marital status, her place of birth, her parentage. He feels attracted and curious about her but decides not to look at her to avoid temptation. The next time he goes to see her in her office to deliver and fix up the board, she removes his defective goggles and touches him in the process. It thrills him and he asks her residential address of an outhouse in the Third Cross, Number Seven and visits her the next evening. She receives him courteously and extends hospitality. He starts taking care of his looks and clothes and the two are drawn too close. However, on the three-week four, he feels provoked by a cart man to attempt a sexual assault on her in the night of their forced sojourn at the road side on their way back home because the bull suffers injury. She feels shocked and becomes uncommunicative and he too apprehends consequences of his crime in the form of arrest and public shame. He does not go to collect his bill from his office. After about a fortnight she visits him at the workshop in the backyard of his house and show her amenability. He starts visiting and sleeping at her place in the night and declares to his aunt that he is marrying Daisy. Her aunt does not approve it because they are Brahmins and Daisy is a Christian name. When Raman insists that he has decided to marry her, his aunt decides to leave on a pilgrimage of Haridwar, Badrinath and Banaras. This disturbs Raman but he does not agree to forget Daisy. He makes arrangements for the aunt's pilgrimage.

After she is gone, he gets the house renovated, scrubbed and whitewashed and removes the images of gods to a cupboard so that the aunt's worship room could be occupied by Daisy exclusively. Daisy does not like gods being locked. Marriage has no place in her scheme of life. She has been ordained by a Christian missionary to serve the cause of Family Planning. She feels affected by increasing population, consequent poverty, ignorance and misery and human degradation. She does not discriminate between rich and the poor, the high and the low. She herself sleeps on a mat on the ground and eats whatever is available, travels by whatever mode is available: taxi, bus, lorry, bullock cart, walking on feet! She does not mind her discomforts and inconveniences. Even at this young age her heels have cracks. She is motivated to do her best for the country: "I like to serve the people in what seems to me the best way, that's all. And in this area allotted to me now, if I can arrest the population growth by even 5 per cent within this year, I'll be satisfied."

She does not believe in marriage forms and styles but agrees Gandharva way because it involves no wastages. She does not need furniture and does not believe in cooking. She repeatedly demonstrates her indifference to Raman's excited narration of the plans for their future. She agrees to shift to Raman's house, however at 8 a.m. on the tenth date next because her lease on her present accommodation would expire that day. But a day before the appointed day she is visited by three women from Nagri to inform her of an alarming rise of 30% in the population in one year in that area. She acts swiftly by summoning medical team from Delhi and decides to shift her working to that area. She declares an end to her relationship with Raman without any apparent show of emotion or concern for his future plans. However, she presses and kisses his land before rushing down to the waiting taxt only to acknowlege his warmth for her.

The *Painter of Signs* demonstrates Narayan's involvement in profound matters. On the face of it, it is the story of a small town signboard painter falling in love with a family planning worker. Both of them spurn marriage as unnecessary and sex as a degrading obsession. Though Raman haggles with customers for a few rupees more or less, offers of a fat sum of five thousand in dowry don't move him. A sexual look at a woman is not to his liking. Obviously he is moulded by ancient philosophic outlook towards sex as degrading hence avoidable. This is in great contrast to the western attitude to have more and more of sex in as weird manner as conceivable. Daisy is not interested in anything except her mission of helping reduce population growth. Before she leaves her parental home and comes under the influence of a Christian missionary she experiences how marriage degrades a woman who is supposed to be always falling at the feet of males as dust. She is not allowed to feel equal or better than her male counterpart even though the latter may be a mere literate and she highly educated and accomplished! This status is not acceptable to her and she sacrifices the comforts, security and respectability of belonging to high class families. She realizes that a woman is used as child-producing device only without any regard for her human dignity. When men have nothing else to do during monsoon days or when harvesting is over, then they indulge in their favourite pastime of impregnating the woman. This is neither acceptable to the new young man nor to the new young woman. The traditional way of looking at the caste, creed and financial status of the groom by the family of the girl and vice versa is no longer valid. Marriage as a commercial bargain is rejected by the new generation and wastages like huge expenses on ceremonies and other ostentations must be avoided by voluntary consent, not by coercion.

# 'A Tiger for Malgudi'

The author was inspired to write this novel after his visit to Kumbha Mela at the confluence of three holiest rivers Ganga, Yamuna and invisible Saraswati at Allahabad. There he saw an unleashed tiger following a hermit without hurting or scaring any one. The writer thought that all books are written with a focus on man and it never occurs to anyone to view animals possessing wisdom, ego, outlook and a desire to communicate. That an animal may also have the instinct to be objective and the capability to rise above the self and think of doing good to others. After his encounter with the unleashed tiger, it occurred to the writer that even an otherwise ferocious animal could also turn an ascetic or withdraw from all temptations. The wild looking animal too could thus, attain heights of thought and meditate upon the meaning and purpose of existence of physical as well as spiritual levels.

Narayan reproduces the story of this tiger as if told by the tiger in its last stage of life at a Zoo. The tiger begins by telling that it was a small cub frolicking under the care of its mother. Then, one day she disappeared leaving it to face the world of the forest. It learnt to survive by hiding, getting "knocked down and hurt by bigger animals and menaced by lesser ones, " (p. 13) by starving and surviving to grow into the Supreme Lord of the Jungle. Now it starts killing and inflicting unthinkable cruelty on weaker creatures. In due course it wins over a tigress, after a ferocious fight and father four cubs. The tigress, however, strays into human habitat in search of prey and soon killed. Trailing their mother the cubs too meet the same fate. The tiger follows them in search and after a few days of panic caused by it in the forest village, it is captured alive in a cage, by a trainer of animals and owner of the Grand Malgudi Circus. After it is captured it is kept hungry for several days to subdue it. It is taught one trick after the other with the poking and dangling of a hunter. Each subsequent trick becomes more difficult and dangerous, hence disliked by it. Soon, however, the tiger discovers the virtue of his new life in captivity. It has to perform according to the dictates of its master once in a day or two and then it is allowed food and rest. There is no competition with any other animal and no botheration of hunting. However, it does not continue for long because in spite of great effort the tiger cannot resist the temptation of eating the goat that drinks milk from a common saucer. The incident is witnessed and photographed by a film producer Madhusudan. The latter starts thinking of making a film in which the hero would knock down the tiger. Madhusudan offers a big sum in contract to the Circus Captain for shooting the film with the tiger cast in it. After several comic developments in which the hero Jaggu runs away when the tiger is brought before him. Raja, the tiger gets irritated at performing the same act of rising on its hind legs to catch a dangling lamb in rehearsals repeatedly. It strikes back when an electric shock is administered to make Raja obey the Captain and walks away to his freedom. The slight brush of Raja's paw proves fatal for the Captain. Now, there is no one who can command Raja. It walks towards the city. There is a stampede wherever it goes. People are panicked to see it walking past them. The school children run back to their school and shut themselves in. Raja enters the Headmaster's room where it is shut in. The Headmaster climbs the attic in panic and Raja takes rest on the ground. Outside there is a great commotion. A hunter

Alphonse comes to shoot it. He is followed by volunteers of the Society for the Prevention of Cruelty to Animals. The Chairman of SPCA, however, agrees to permit Alphonse to kill it, after getting some hush money. Alphonse is actually a trader in tiger skins. All this while there is an ascetic present who is ridiculed and whose advice persistently ignored by the vested interests. However, Alphonse develops cold feel at the actual moment of shooting. The ascetic comes forward and on his assurance that the tiger would not harm any one, it is allowed to walk out of the headmaster's room.

This ascetic is no other than a former resident of Ellaman Street of Malgudi. His name began with G. either Govind, Gopal or Gund and he used to rush about on his bicycle up the Market Road, as a student of B.A. As a patriotic young man he took active part in the freedom movement and was arrested for tearing down the British flag from the roof of the District Collector's office. Then he disappeared after leaving his wife and children in the manner of Siddhartha. It is rumoured that he went to the Himalayas and attained pure knowledge before coming back to Malgudi. After the door of the headmaster's room is opened, Raja walks out after an initial show of rage displayed in dashing its head in all the possible directions of the ascetic's presence. The ascetic knows the language of the animals besides ten human languages. He conveys to the tiger the need to forgo violence in order to be civilized. The tiger and his new master, thus proceed through the streets of the town. People stop their activities and those quarrelling run away. The two reach a "spot on a ledge jutted over by a rock for a stay." (p. 157) The hermit discourses to the tiger that its exterior has no relation to its interior. However, he tells the tiger to go hunting in order to satisfy its physical hunger since he could do nothing about it. He meditates here and occasionally enlightens the tiger about God, soul, the purpose of life and the need to detach from worldly things and affairs. He also explains that God is everywhere and each one of us, man and animal alike, sees Him only in one's image. One must not have a negative outlook on life or towards others and should try to have an enlarged vision, beyond one's narrow definitions. One of these is the use of numbers that has added to the misery of man. The habit of "looking forward or backward or waiting" also distracts our concentration from the present. The sage further demonstrates that one must not inflate one's ego under flattery from others. At the last stage the great soul tells the tiger that they must part since the former's time in the world was over the soon the tigger would also die thereafter. Since it would not be proper for him to leave the tiger disciple unattended in the forest with all its wild habits and needs drastically modified, the hermit arranges for its transportation to zoo.

Here there would be no tasks to perform and no danger of harm from any human or animal. The tiger would be well looked after as if leading the life of retirement awaiting departure for a new life.

As Narayan grows in age, he becomes more spiritual and inwardly. The novel *A Tiger for Malgudi* is a clear evidence of this progression in the thinking of the novelist. He leaves behind the mundane issues of love, marriage, money-making, occupations, social bullying and the like. The prominent national issues like family planning and women's education too become secondary. Now is the time to meditate upon and look into the problems of physical and spiritual existence as also man's relation to other creatures around. He finds that man's ego has alienated him not only from man but has created a deep chasm between man and animal. This also means that he has distanced himself from Nature, the common mother of us all. Because of this drift his understanding of God has remained inadequate and distorted too. He progresses on his way to physical and mental development by increasing his knowledge. However, he has not been able to assimilate the vast amount of knowledge gathered by him. This has resulted in distorted perception of his relationship vis-a-vis the rest of Nature. He has shrouded himself with the delusion that he is the supreme master. Under this belief he has subjugated his fellow men, animals and other inanimate objects. He has forgotten the Supreme Creator since he considers himself the creator and destroyer to all the things in the world. The height of absurdity can be witnessed in man's image, conception and attributes of God as identical with man's. This fallacy is easily entertainable because he possesses powers unsurpassable by any other animal. Besides, he possesses great physical force which he can manipulate, deploy and enhance as per the needs of the occasion. The other animals like tiger, elephant too have vast physical strength in their bodies but they lack the facility of a dynamic deployment of it under varying circumstances. A judicious combination of physical and mental strengths has placed man on the top of the hierarchy of the physical world. However, this combination and achievement have led him astray from the natural and desirable path. He covets more than what he needs and destroys even that which does not harm him. This unjustifiable greed and destructive tendency have become alarming source of peril to his own existence.

Narayan has chosen to articulate his opinion on matters of existence through a tiger. This is symbolical of man's present predicament. The tiger is fierce and powerful, yet it does not kill more than what it needs. It goes on feeding upon the stale and stinking carcass till it has flesh upon it. The next attempt is made only when the need arises and not before. Its downfall begins with its entrapment in sex that leads to its bondage through its progeny. It is happy working in the circus because it has a sort of discipline that demands performance and rewards it with food and rest. The performance is hard work not exactly to his great liking but hard work nevertheless.

It is along the earlier pattern in the forest except that now the tiger is not so much accountable for its acts as it used to be in the forest. There is a certain amount of dignity in the circus and when it is violated, the tigerishness is revoked, the discipline that is being instilled is put aside and the tiger reverts back to its Nature, as is demonstrated in the tiger eating the goat while drinking the milk from the same bowl at the same time. The man refuses to learn lessons from Nature which keeps reminding him of avoiding to indulge excesses. The consequences of ignoring Nature's caution are always serious. The case of Captain cannot be an exception. He too refuses to learn from the circus goat experience and pays by the life when his greed compels him to break the limits of tolerance of the tiger in inducing it to chase the dangling limb. The tiger, i.e., the entrapped vital force within, has vast potential for doing good in any cause provided it is deployed judiciously. The unrestricted human greed has been leading to increased doses of miseries and yet man does not learn his lesson.

It has resulted in misery to man more than it has damaged Nature. Nature is a self rejuvenating force because it consumes the minimum while it yields the maximum. On the one hand it is 'red in tooth and claw' while it has its own system of harmonious checks and balances. Man is out of tune with the harmony which must be restored. Narayan, therefore, suggests through the tiger's example that it has the same divine existence within as man boasts of for himself but enjoys violating it at every step and blames external forces for his arrogance. Zoologists also affirm that all animals act similarly because each creature is apprehensive of the conduct of the other. Every offensive action on the part of every animal is, therefore, an exercise of its fundamental right to life. Man alone indulges in violating this right of all others without much cause and justification. Its root cause is his unlimited greed.

Raising the level of consciousness is, therefore, the basic need of mankind. Such men, as the hermit master of the tiger, have been able to develop a dignified look at all the objects around, are easily identifiable by a haze or glow that surrounds them. This glow emanates borne of a sense and conviction of a positive outlook at the universe as a whole that forbids him to commit injustice at anyone. The key to man's real happiness lies, therefore, in righteous conduct that would promote a great sense of objectivity in him. Narayan seems to ask through the narrative of *A Tiger for Malgudi* that if a wild ferocious tiger could learn to modify his basic nature and seek his satisfaction in asceticism, what prevents man from simply reverting to his original state of doling out happiness to all.

The tragedy of the situation, as Narayan has rightly perceived, is that the more the man acquires and attains, the more foul uses of his acquisitions and attainments he makes. The simple folk are called ignorant and wretched because they have no inclination to play foul. They are simply onlookers of any situation, good or evil. This is evident in the ordinary men's panic at the sight of the unleashed tiger. They are easily persuaded, however, to shed off their fear of the tiger walking on streets but led by a self-disciplined man, i.e., the hermit.

# 'Talkative Man'

*Talkative Man* (Penguin, 1986) is TM or T Madhu is freelance reporter. He has made his place important in the society of Malgudi. His credentials are excellent and his reputation is high. He lives in his big ancestral bungalow on Kabir Street, which is the only aristocrats' locality besides Ellaman Street. It is known for its lofty and patronising hospitality."[1] Madhu is better known as a Talkative Man in the manner of the epical Narada who must talk and spread gossips without which he cannot remain at ease. His favourite squatting place is his friend Varma's The Boardless Hotel. He has a special chair reserved for him facing a calender with the picture of demon Mahishasur. Varma is a devoted listener and is enchanted by a story about one Dr. Rann told by TM over several weeks.

Dr. Rann is actually Rangan from a village Maniyar. He has trimmed it into a foreign sounding name Rann. He has blonde hair, greenish-blue eyes and borderline complexion. These features make him a cross-breed of the local woman with some European colonial soldier in India. He claims to be associated with United Nations Development Project and has a UN passport. On its strength he has visited several countries like Rhodesia, Kuwait. He comes to Malgudi to collate the enormous data collected in Timbuctoo. He declares that he has come to Malgudi because it is peaceful place where he can write his report and another important book. He lodges himself in the waiting-room at the railway station because he has not found suitable lodgings in the town. He learns about Madhu as a resourceful person and waits for him in the latter's chair in the Reading Room in Lawley Memorial Library. Rann requests Madhu to help him find a suitable place for his stay and save him from the bed-bugs and mosquitoes of the railways waiting room. His tastes are high and living standards are European. No place is therefore, found suitable for his stay in Malgudi. Ultimately TM lodges him in his own house which is large and lies unused because there are no members in his household. Rann grumbles about the lack of basic facilities here too but adapts to changed conditions gradually. He hires furniture for his use, to give away the impression that he has no intention to go. One day it occurs to TM that he should write an article on the privileged presence of Rann as an important international personality in Malgudi. Soon, however, the newspaper demands a photograph of the person to be published along side the article. He is photographed without his knowledge in accordance with a plan executed by TM in agreement with his photographer friend Jayaraj. The publication of the photograph, however, brings 'a six foot woman....dark complexioned, cropped head and in jeans and a T-shirt with bulging breasts.'[2] She is bold and very dominant type of a woman. She says that she had been seduced by Rann and enticed to marry him in spite of her parents' disapproval and obstruction. They got him arrested for kidnapping a minor girl and forced her to state in the court that she had been abducted by Rann. The case was dismissed in favour of Rann but he never felt happy thereafter with the conduct of Roja, the Punjabi carpentry-shop owner of Madras. He soon deserted her.

The story of the Commandant Sarasa of Home Guards Women's Auxiliary of Delhi does not however, move TM to betray his friend. He saves his guest and dispatches the lady. Soon, however, he is alarmed to learn that his guest is indulging the same game with the teenage grand daughter of the librarian of Lawley Memorial Library. The old man has been very kind to him and the young girl is inexperienced of the wicked ways of persons like Rann. He has been taking her in TM's taxi-driver friend Gaffur's taxi to a cemetery where he works the magic of his love talk on the young raw female. He has already made plans to elope with her. TM, therefore, decides to act. He calls his former wife and arranges a public lecture by Rann. A Deputy Minister is invited to preside over this programme at the lotus club. It generates lots of publicity and a huge crowd responds. The police is also present because of the minister's presence. The minister, however, leaves after his speech. There is lots of hackling when Rann starts speaking. Lights are switched off and Rann is advised to exit to safety in a car waiting outside. Actually Rann's wife, together with her accomplices, is waiting for him in that car. He is taken by her to her house. Soon, however, he elopes with a nurse Komal from Matilda's. Rann had actually used the facilities of his stay with his wife Rosa to develop love-relationship with an unsuspecting nurse Komal. He is a lady-killer and has cast his spell on many an unsupecting woman including "Mary, Rita, Nancy, Manu, Kamala and so on."[3]

In the short-long story of *Talkative Man,* Narayan has chosen to elaborate the menacing disease of seducing young girls by unscrupulous men. These men are very pleasant and submissive looking. They talk their way to the hearts of the young girls. They are careful to locate girls belonging to prosperous families only. The teenage girls have no experience of the wicked ways of the world. They fall prey to the rosy pictures of high promises of a dream life of luxuries and successes painted by these young men. The effect of rosy talk on the raw minds and hearts of such teenagers is so great that they do not consult any elderly person and consider their parents as their enemies. They believe everything said by their so-called lovers. They decide to desert their parents on the strength of promises made by young strangers. Such seducers are not content with deceiving one or two girls but one after the other until they are caught. However, they are incorrigible.

*The Talkative Man* is an advancement over all the earlier novels of Narayan. It has been written around the dogmatic efforts of one woman Roja alias Sarasa. She chases Rann in his flight away from her. She succeeds in catching hold of him in a great dramatic manner. Though Narayan compares her efforts with those of mythological Savitri's to rescue her husband Satyavan from the clutches of the god of Death, the comparison is not justified because Satyavan is not known to be a bad character. He was simply helpless before Death. This narrative has the elements of mock-heroic, however. Rann is in the business of regularly deceiving young unmarried girls. He changes his identity and place every time he succeeds in hooking on to a new girl. When he is successful in winning over a new girl to elope with him, he starts looking for his next victim. He is just like the poisonous and menacing weed called Cannibal Herb that does not allow growth of any healthy plant.

*The Talkative Man* seems to focus on the problem of deception of young maidens by unscrupulous but decent looking men. However, it records corruption in other forms too. The Station Master boasts of his unblemished record and asks Rann to vacate the waiting room only to blackmail the passenger into bribing. Once his plam is greased, no rules seem to be violated. The old librarian is a retired sheristedar at the district courts. He earned lots of money in exchange for favours to the litigants besides the judge who too "accepted bribes chanelled through the sheristedar."[4]

Once again we are delighted to observe the growth of Malgudi. Albert Mission School has become a college now. In its drive towards modernization, it has acquired the autorickshaws. Of course, these are not many and their new pliers lack etiquette of the trade. Still, its use is a sign of status. Scooters are already used by inhabitants here. A modern sanitaryware shop sells modern fittings of toilets and bathrooms. The town is known for its tranquility and even foreigners prefer to stay here and dispose off their pending work in the peaceful atmosphere here. However, Malgudi cannot remain untouched by the vices that flourish in big cities. So, smuggling and narcotics and the Interpol too can be felt here. The citizens cannot, therefore, remain content with their simple ways. They must become smart enough to face the dangers from glib-tongued, well-paying men's dubious ways. They may pose themselves as foreigners by affecting alien tone and clothing and westernized life styles while they may be basically Indians. Rann is no other than Rangan. He is in the habit of assuming a new identity every time he cheats. He has been Ashok, Naren, D'Cruz, John, Adam, Shankar, Sridhar, Singh and Iqbal becoming Rann. National or religious considerations have no significance for such people. They are not communal in their approach. The flexibility with which Rann changes his name in consonance with the identity of his spotted victim is admirable. His credentials in this respect are highly secular. It is possible that TM signifies a graduation in the thinking of Narayan. Through Rann he may be hinting at the emergence of a new breed of self-centred youngmen whose only aim is to enjoy the pleasures of life without any inhibition. Their counterpart should, therefore, be women like Roja. She is independent, bold, courageous and indefatigable. It appears Narayan presents her as a model for Indian womanhood. Gone are the days of sulking Rukmini.

The small angels of Malgudi like the porter, the taxi-driver, fat Ramu the neighbour, automan Kari and the last saved girl Girija must change with the times and put up smarter airs. If they continue to ignore the rapid changes in the conduct of the people from urban settings, they would continue to suffer perils to their careers and lives.

# 'The World of Nagaraj'

Gopu and Nagaraj are the two sons of an aristocratic inheritor of vast rice fields and other residential properties. They live in the posh Kabir Street. Gopu, the elder is married to Charu after his graduation. He is not interested in any kind of employment and spurns suggestions and efforts of his father. He begets a son Krishnaji, affectionately called Tim. After Nagaraj completes his graduation, he too is married to Sita, daughter of a retired government servant. No child is born to them in spite of all the treatments available. They shower their affections on Tim from his infanthood. After the death of father, Gopu divides the properties and all the assets leaving the present residence and mother for Nagaraj. He keeps the fields and other valuables for himself and moves over to the village with his family. He is very serious about agricultural operations and sets up a gobar gas plant, uses fertilizers, pesticides and talks of acquiring machinery and a tractor too. Tim, however, is not interested in this garbage business and walks out one day on the pretext of his father calling him 'donkey'. He comes to live with Nagaraj permanently. Nagaraj buys him a bicycle and envisions of papers, books on Tim's table. Things settle down and Gopu feels reconciled to Tim's education. Nagaraj and Charu pamper Tim and delight in waiting upon him. He rises late and avoids Nagaraj but goes to Sita for all his needs. He starts borrowing the scooter of the Nagaraj's friend the Talkative Man. He also starts frequenting Kismet the newly opened liquor bar and comes home late and drunk. When questioned about the smell, he tells Nagaraj that his friends had sprayed eu-de-cologne. Nagraja's worries are further compounded when he discovers that Tim has not been going to the school since the beginning of the term. Tim also tells him of winning a lottery. However, Gopu comes the next morning and discloses about match for Tim with Delhi settled family of Trichi. Nagaraj and Sita are worried at this development and decide to inform Gopu. After marriage of Tim with Saroja they occupy the same middle room in which Gopu had lived after his marriage. Now there are loud gigglings readings and singings in accompaniment with harmonium.

Tim is attached and very sensitive about his wife. He cannot bear with any body showing no regard for her talent. She has started singing and playing harmonium at the club. Once when Nagaraj leaves in the middle of her singing, he leaves home and goes to live at the club. There again, when the Secretary replaces her instrument with a legged one, he beats him and leaves the club and comes back to Nagaraj and starts living as if he had never left.

Nagaraj has his friends Coomar, a sari business man. He helps him with a capital of two hundred to start the door to door sale of saris. After Coomar's business flourishes, Nagaraj agrees to write his accounts regularly. His another friend is a journalist called Talkative Man. The primary obsession of Nagaraj is to write a grand book on the mythological wandering sage Narada. However, he is worried because of non-availability of authentic material on Narada. He approaches Kavu pandit who declines at the beginning but agrees on the intervention of Talkative Man. Kavu Pandit, however, keeps postponing the beginning of lesson on one pretext or the other like his busyness in the morning puja, his rest hour in the afternoon, waiting for the auspicious moment to begin. Nagaraj feels harassed and realises that this man is befooling him even though he has paid him the fee in advance. Later Talkative Man informs him that Kavu Pandit is a gambler on playing cards and that is the only item of his interest. His search for authentic information/material on Narad takes him. to Bari next, the north Indian stationary seller from Aligarh. Bari claims that *Narad Puran* is his family heirloom and Nagaraj is welcome to take notes from the readings of the sacred book. However, after several days of readings by Bari, there is no mention of the name of Narada. Nagaraj postpones his grand plan of writing his book on Narada because he realizes that the problems created by Tim, Saroja and Gopu are more urgent.

Tim has left home with Saroja. They have started living in the outhouse of the club. Saroja sings and plays harmonium every evening on a payment of fifty rupees. Tim is annoyed with both Nagaraj and Gopu that he refuses to talk to them when approached on road. He disappears with a shopping bag on his shoulders in a very dirty locality. Gopu chases him and sits on dharna to demand to see his son. He knocks down the club strongmen when they try to remove him on the orders of the office bearers. However, when Gopu learns that Tim does not want to see him, he goes back disillusioned to his village.

*The World of Nagaraj* offers a rare glimpse of the slow degeneration of the traditionally wealthy class. They have no love or regard for education. They are not interested in any career or profession except enjoying life at the cost of the labour of others. For them agriculture is lucrative because there they have ample opportunity to lord over the poor, illiterate workers. For this reason alone they like to live in rural setting. The urban settings hold no charm for them because here they have to be restrained, trained and skilled in modern ways and outlook. However, the traditional aristocrat behaves queerly even in urban settings. Nagaraj is a graduate. This qualifies him for marriage. He does not feel the necessity to earn his living because his parents have left enough for him. He must keep himself busy so he loiters here and there gossiping with a journalist friend of his school days or writing accounts for another businessman friend Commar, without seeking or receiving remuneration. His larger obsession is to write a book on the mythical sage Narada. His justification for seeking to write this look is that no one has attempted to do it so far. He has no child of his own, so he virtually adopts his brother's son and pampers by supplying all these needs and bearing with all his demands, whether reasonable or undesirable. He takes life so easily that he always shies away from questioning and demanding a reasonably satisfactory answer from anyone. He does not assert because, perhaps, he is conscious of the aimlessness of his own existence. He has received everything without suffering for it. He is free of the anxiety of supplying the daily needs. He does not suffer for his children because he has none of his own but has the gap filled by a son who is as good as his own. He has not bothered to chalk out a career for himself, so he does not mind much if his nephew Tim goes to left or to the right. However, this is not his individual weakness but that of his class. His elder brother Gopu is a little more sensible because he takes full interest in everything with which he is concerned. He modernises agricultural operations. Though Tim has been hijacked by his younger brother, Gopu still feels anxious about him and keeps track of all that the boy does. Like a responsible parent, he fixes a match for the son when he realises that the boy has grown big and started boozing and frequenting bars and clubs. Drinking, clubs and songs and dances are the major preoccupations of the wealthy class. They don't have to worry about their two meals. If they have no such vices, then asceticism, going to the extreme of eccentricities like wearing ochre clothes for worship in the morning, wandering here and there to look for sources of information on the wandering mythological sage Narada or writing accounts of a businessman for free, are indulged in by them. All this points out to a serious lack of vision and purpose in their lives.

Narayan's latest novel *The World of Nagaraj* is another step in the direction of identifying the purpose for life. The earlier step, *A Tiger for Malgudi* is also an attempt to focus on the meaning of life. In the earlier book he discourses upon the righteousness and objective virtues and the desirability of a positive outlook on life. It appears that Narayan has tried to elaborate that point by showing, in contrast, that a life lived in emptiness, as is done by Nagaraj, is more cumbersome than a life lived in accordance with the dictats of one's nature and instincts. This is illustrated by the example of the tiger. At the opening of the novel we find Nagaraj calls himself a man of mission but looks away when questioned about the nature of his mission. His obsession with Narada speaks of his vagrant and aimless life. As Narada is never steady, so is Nagaraj. Narada has no purpose and is present anywhere, any time, welcome or not. So is Nagaraj. He is not interested in a steady job, so he volunteers to be the accountant of his friend Commar. The latter used his discretion in recovering or postponing recoveries of debts but Nagaraj is worried about the Public Prosecutor's account. He would not have allowed his own son to do what he tolerates in Tim. Nagaraj is a man who has no locus standie vis a vis anyone, anything or any affair, yet he wants to give away the impression of being important. No body takes him seriously. Tim and Gopu don't take cognizance of his presence. Tim goes a step further when he tells him that the smell of liquor from his mouth is actually that of eu-de-cologne. This is within Nagaraj's reckoning: Did the boy take him to be an idiot? Just because he was old-fashioned and moved about in dhoti and shirt and upper cloth instead of pants and bush Shirt?" (p. 82) Here too Nagaraj is trying to be naive because the looks and attire of a person do not make much difference if he has an awakened mind. Nagaraj acts like a street dog that goes sniffing and pissing at every step and corner, barks where there is none but whines when confronted by an adversary. Anyone who takes a fancy or finds a use for him is welcome to rope him in. Coomar, the astute businessman ties him at his shop door by placing a chair and asking him to write accounts and make suggestions. Kavu pandit and Bari both consider him a fool who has lots of time and money too but no guts to find out who is who. Even his wife Sita is aware of his weak character. She exhorts him to be firm in questioning Tim about late night return and liquor smell, because it is his responsibility to ensure Tim does not go wayward since he is being brought up by him like his own son. But, he does not have the courage to assert himself and the boy goes past him onto his bicycle. He does not feel angry even after learning that Tim has not gone to the school since the beginning of the Term. On the contrary he heaves a sigh of relief after Tim tells him that he has won a small amount in lottery, in company with his friends. In stead of feeling outraged at the boy taking to gambling as a career, he feels consoled that his prospects are bright.

As usual, there are lots of comic-ironic situations in this novel too. Nagaraj accepts the advice of an ascetic to wear ochre coloured clothes when meditating for an hour and informs him that he has been living with his wife as if with a sister. When his mother calls him Nagu, he retorts by mumbling that he was a 52 year old man and the mother treats him as if he were a boy. Bari repeatedly emphasises upon crow-brand notebooks and his readings from the *Narad Puran* without a mention of Narad for days with the retort that Narad had not been born yet, are pure delight. Kavu Pandit's argument that he must find out an auspicious moment to seek an auspicious moment" (p. 115) for a beginning, is a superb piece of irony upon too much fuss about astrological configurations and their role in regulating the modern man's fast moving life.

The novel records further growth of Malgudi. It is sad to note that now there have opened bars and clubs where liquor, singing and presumably dancing girls dominate the scene. Malgudi has so far witnessed healthy growth. Though there have been labour, slum and hygeine problems due to rapid industrialisation and expansion, it has been free of the modern centres of vice like bars and clubs where women of decent families are gradually enticed to come and perform. This is the beginning of the disintegration of family life. Tim's walking out of this situation is not due to his disapproval but his failure to fully reconcile with and take a plunge in the flow of modernity. His permanent withdrawal from the club is symbolical of the rejection of this trend of culture. He does not regret his decision and never mentions his days at the bar and the club. He is unaffected by whatever happened as in a nightmare.

# Bibliography


**Primary Works of RK Narayan**

*Swami and Friends.* London: Hamish Hamilton, 1935.

*The Bachelor of Arts.* London: Netson, 1937.

*The Dark Room.* London: Macmillan, 1938.

*The English Teacher.* (U.S. edition: Grateful to Life and Death) London: Eyre and Spottiswoode, 1945.

*Mr. Sampath.* London: Eyre and Spottswoode, 1949.

*The Financial Expert.* London: Methuen, 1955.

*Waiting for the Mahatma.* London: Methuen, 1955.

*The Guide.* London: The Bodley Head, 1958.

*The Man Eater of Malgudi.* London: Heinemann, 1962.

*The Sweet Vendor.* (Indian edition: The Vendor of Sweets) London: The Bodely Head, 1967.

*The Painter of Signs.* New York: The Viking Press, 1967.

*A Tiger for Malgudi.* Mysore: Indian Thought Publications.

*Talkative Man.* London: Penguin, 1986.

*The World of Nagaraj.* Mysore: Indian Thought Publications.

*Malgudi Days.* Mysore: Indian Thought Publications, 1943.

*Dodu and Other Stories.* Mysore: ITP, 1943.

*Cyclone and Other Stories.* Mysore: ITP, 1944.

*An Astrologer's Day and Other Stories.* Mysore: ITP, 1947.

*Lawley Road*. Mysore: ITP, 1956.

*A House and Two Goats*. New York: The Viking Press, 1970.

*Old and New*. Mysore: ITP, 1981.

**Other Writings of Narayan**

*The Watchman of the Laker* (One Act Play). Mysore: ITP, 1940.

*Next Sunday* (Essays and Sketches). ITP, 1956.

*My Dateless Dairy* (Travelogue). ITP, 1960.

*Gods, Demons and Other* (Indian Mythological Stories retold) New York: The Viking Press, 1964.

*The Ramayana*. New York: The Viking Press, 1972.

*Reluctant Guru* (Essays and Sketches). Delhi: Hind Pocket Books, 1974.

*Mahabharat*. New York: The Viking Press, 1978.

"The Fiction Writer in India: His Tradition and His Problem." *The Atlantic Monthly*. Oct. 1935.

"On the Abuse of Criticism", *Literary Criticism: European and Indian Traditions*. Ed. C D Narasimaiah. Mysore: University of Mysore, 1965.

"The Word of Story Teller," *Fiction and the Reading Public in India. Ed.* CD Narasimaiah. Mysore: UMP 1967.

"Misguided Guide." *Life*. 15 May 1967.

"Gods Demons and Modern Times." *The Literary Criterion*. Mysore, 1972.

**Secondary Sources**

Anniah Gowda, H.H. "The Comic Muse and RK Narayan" *Kakatiya Journal of English Studies*. Warangal, 1978.

Argyle, Barry, "Narayan's The Sweet Vendor," *The Journal of Commonwealth Literature*, June 1972.

Berry, Margaret, "R K Narayan: Lila and Literature." *Journal of English Writing in English.* July 1976.

Biswal, Jayant K.A. *Critical Study of the Novels of R.K. Narayan,* New Delhi: Nirmal Publishers, 1987.

Chellapan, K. "Double Consciousness in the Novels of R K Narayan." *Scholar Critic,* Jan. 1981.

Deva, Soma, *R.K. Narayan's The Guide: A Critical Study,* Bareilly: Prakash Book Depot, 1973

Gerebian, Keith. "Narayan's Compromise in Comedy." *The Literary Half-Yearly.* Mysore. Jan. 1976.

Gerow, Edwin. "The Quintessential Narayan." *Literature East and West.* 1966.

Ghai, T.C. "Pattern and Significance in RK Narayan's Novels." *Indian Literature.* Jul-Sep. 1975.

Goud, L M. "Indianism in the works of R K Narayan." *Experimentation of Language in Indian Writing in English.* Ed. S.K. Desai. Kolhapur: Shivaji University, 1974.

Goyal, Bhagwat S. "R.K. Narayan: *A Critical Spectrum*". Meerut: Sthalabh Book House, 1983.

Hartley, Louis. "In Malgudi with R K Narayan." *Literature East and West,* 1956.

Holmstorm, Lakshmi. *The Novels of R.K. Narayan,* Calcutta: Writers' Workshop, 1973.

Kaul, A.N. "R.K. Narayan and East West Theme," *Indian Literature,* 1972.

Kantak, V Y. "The Achievement of R K Narayan," *Indian Literature in the Past Fifty Years.* Ed. C D Narasimhaiah. Mysore: University of Mysore, 1970.

Mehta, Ved. "The Train Had Just Arrived at Malgudi Station." *John is Easy to Please.* Penguin 1967.

Malhotra, Tara. "Old places, Old Faces, Old Tunes: A Critical Study of Narayan's Latest Fiction," *The Banasthali Patrika*, Vol. 13, 1969.

Krishnan, S. "A Day With R K Narayan." *Span*, April 1975.

Mishra, G. "The Holyman in R.K. Narayn's Novels, "*Journal of Literary Studies*, Vol. II, No. 2, Dec. 1979.

Mukerji, Nirmal. "Some Aspects of the Literary Development of R.K. Narayan," *Banasthali Patrika*, Vol. 13, July 1969.

Murti, K.V.S. "The Theme of Salvation: Mulk Raj Anand and R.K. Narayan," *Triveni*, Vol. 34, Oct. 1965.

———, "Theme and Form in R.K. Narayan's *The Man Eater of Malgudi*," *The Journal of Commonwealth Literature*, Vol. 10, No. 3, April 1976.

Naik, M.K. *The Ironic Vision: A Study of the Fiction of R.K. Narayan*, New Delhi: Sterling Publications, 1983.

Narayan, Surendra. "The Ironic Mode of R K Narayan." *Indian Writing in English*. Ed. K.N. Sinha. New Delhi: Heritage Publishers, 1975.

Nasimi, R.A. *The Language of Mulk Raj Anand, Raja Rao, and R.K. Narayan*. Delhi Capital Publishing House, 1989.

Nirupama Rani, K "Autobiographical Element in R.K. Narayan's early Novels," *Triveni*, Vol. 45, No. 3, Oct-Dec. 1976.

Malhotra, Tara. "Old Places, Old Faces, Old Tunes," *The Banasthali Patika* July 1969.

Panduranga Rao, V. "The Art of R K Narayan." *The Journal of Commonwealth Literature*. July 1968.

"The Craftsmanship of R.K. Narayan." *Indian Writing in English*. Ed. Ramesh Mohan. Bombay: Orient Longman. 1978.

———, "Tea With R.K. Narayan." *The Journal of Commonwealth Literature*, July 1971.

Prasad, Sharda. "R.K. Narayan, Writer and Novelist." *Traveller in India*, Summer 1969.

Raghavacharulu, DVK. "Naipaul and Narayan: The Sense of Life." *Awakened Conscience: Studies in Commonwealth Literature.* Ed. CD Narasimhaiah. New Delhi: Sterling, 1978.

Raizada, H. *R.K. Narayan: A Critical Study of His Works.* New Delhi: Young India Publications, 1969.

Rajeev, Taranath. "The Average as Positive." *Critical Essays on Indian Literature in English.* Eds. MK Naik, SK Desai and GS Amur. Dharwar: Karnataka Univ., 1968.

Ram, Atma. Ed. *Perspectives on R.K. Narayan*, Ghaziabad: Vimal Prakashan, 1981.

Ranganath, N. "Realism in Literature: A Critique of R.K. Narayana's *The Guide*," *Triveni*, Vol. 487, No. 3, Oct. Dec., 1979.

Rao, Vimla. "The Woman Question in RK Narayan's Novel." *Littcrit.* 1980.

Soma, Krishna. "Towards Serenity: Pattern in the Novels of R.K. Narayan," *The Rajasthan Journal of English Studies*, Nos. 3&4, 1981.

Singh, Natwar. "Tribute to R.K. Narayan." *Quest.* Oct. 1956.

Singh, R.S. *The Guide: Some Aspects.* Delhi: Doaba House, 1971.

Singh, Satyanarayan. "*The Guide:* Crisis and Resolution," *Kakatiya Journal of English Studies*, Vol. 3, No. 1, 1978.

Sivaramakrishna, M. "The Cave and the Temple: Structural Symbolish in *the Guide*," *Osmania Journal of English Studies*, Vol. XIV. No. 1, 1978.

Sundaram, P.S. *R.K. Narayan.* New Delhi: Arnold Heinamann 1973.

Sundaram, P.S. "Malgudi: The World of R.K. Narayan." *The Indian PEN, 1970.*

Updike, John. "R.K. Narayan: A Writer Immersed in His Material." *Span,* April 1979.

Venkatachari, K. "R.K. Narayan's Novels: Acceptance of Life," *Indian Literature,* Vol. III, 1970

Verghese, C. Paul. "R.K. Narayan: His Mind and Art," *Thought,* Vol. 22, No. 28, 11 July 1970.

Walsh, William. *R.K. Narayan: A Critical Appreciation.* London: Heinamann, 1982.

———, "The Intricate Alliance." *Review of English Literature.* Oct. 1961.

———, "Sweet Mangoes and Malt Vinegar." *The Listener.* March 1962.

———, "R.K. Narayan," *Pragati,* Spring 1967.

———, "R.K. Narayan: A Manifold Voice." *Studies in Commonwealth Literature.* London: Chatto and Windus, 1970.

Westbrook, Percy D. "The Short Stories of R.K. Narayan." *Journal of Commonwealth Literature.* July 1968.

William, H.M. "R.K. Narayan and R.P. Jhabwala: Two Interpretations of Modern India." *Literature East and West,* Vol. 16, No. 4, 1972.

Wolseley, R.E. "Narayan of India." *The Nation.* 3 Oct. 1953.

Trivedi, HC and Soni, NK. "Narayan's Dateless Dairy." *The Journal of Indian Writing in English.* Jan. 1979.

Alphonso, Karkala, John B. "Symbolism in the Financial Expert." *Indian Writing Today.* Jan-March 1970.

Sivaramakrishna, M. "Fantasy in *The Financial Expert.*" *The Osmania Journal of English Studies.* 1972.

Bhatanagar, O.P. "Playing the Role in *The Guide* and the Inner Door." *Commonwealth Quarterly*. Dec. 1979.

Naik, MK. "Two Uses of Irony: VS Naipaul's *The Mystic Masseur* and R.K. Narayan's *The Guide." The World Literature Written in English.* Nov. 1978.

Narasimhaiah, CD. "R.K. Narayan's *The Guide." Aspects of Indian Writing in English.* Ed. MK Naik. Delhi: Macmillan, 1979.

Prasad, Pramod, "The Interaction of Romance and Reality in RK Narayan's *The Guide." Indian Writing in English.* Ed Naik. Delhi: Macmillan, 1979.

Singh, R.S. *The Guide: Some Aspects*. Delhi: Doaba House, 1971.

Singh, Satyanarain. "*The Guide:* Crisis and Resolution." *Kakatiya Journal of English Studies*. 1978.

Sivaramakrishna, M. "The Cave and the Temple: Structural Symbolism in The Guide." *Osmania Journal of English Studies. 1978.*

Naik, M.K. "Theme and Form in R.K. Narayan's *The Man-Eater of Malgudi." Journal of Commonwealth Literature,* April 1976.

———, "RK Narayan's *The Painter of Signs:* The Signs are all There." *World Literature written in English*. April, 1972.

# Raja Rao

Raja Rao (1909) was born in a Brahim family in Mysore. The family later moved from Mysore to Hyderabad where he did his schooling. However, his weak lungs prompted his shifting to Aligarh for higher education. He left India on scholarship for Sorbonne University, France to write his Ph.D. on the Influence of Indian Thought on the Mysticism of the West, and Irish literature in particular. He married a French school teacher Camille Mouly who persuaded him to write stories in his native language Kannada rather than in a mixture of Macaulay Yeats-Tagore English. She also developed great interest in Hinduism. However, his marriage with Camille Mouly was dissolved in 1949. He later married an American stage actress Katherine Jones.

During the Thirties he travelled in India, from ashram to ashram, met Mahatma Gandhi and found a Guru in Trivandrum around 1944. Its echoes are found in *The Serpent and the Rope*. He also meditated for three weeks in a temple in Ujjain. While in Benaras, he locked himself away to resolve his dilemma to become a Sanyassin by renouncing the world.

He has rewritten *Kanthapura* (1947); *The Cow of the Barricades and Other Stories* (1947); *The Serpent and the Rope* (1960); *The Cat and Shakespeare* (1965); *Comrade Kirillov* (1976); *The Policeman and the Rose* (1978); *The Chessmaster and His Moves* (1988); *On the Ganga Ghat* (1989). He was awarded Sahitya Akadami Award (1964); *Padma Bhushan* (1969) and Neustadt International Prize for Literature (1988).

India, like any other object and issue, needs to be observed and probed not only from within and without but from a distance too. Curiously, this distant probe is offered in the fiction of Raja Rao. He is a Brahmin, the class of people devoted to the pursuit of learning and knowledge. The Indian Brahmin must live on charity in order to be above temptation and covetousness and also in order to be able to devote himself whole heartedly to the pursuit of the knowledge of the universe. It is society's most sanctified obligation to supply his basic needs so that he may not be distracted from his path. The Indian Brahmin is highly respected as a selfless holyman who commands the confidence borne on reason, enlightenment and utter self-lessness. With the passing of time practice becomes institutionalized and privilege becomes a right.

However, the basic attitude and traits can be discerned. The external manifestation of this Brahminic attitude is found in the practice of untouchability imposed upon a large part of Indian populace, particularly in the south where it is very rigidly observed and segregation, deprivation and denial that automatically go with it. However, for some, Brahminism is a trade mark under which substandard goods can also be supplied while for some others it has become a license to practise frauds and atrocities upon the lowly.

Raja Rao's fiction depicts both these aspects of Brahminic existence in South India. On the one hand the pariahs are made to live on the outskirts of the village because they are the lowest of the lowly untouchables while on the other their lands are bought 'for a song' by the same high class of people, in auction. The novel *Kanthapura* highlights how immature and prankish Brahmain boy Moorthy leads the poor untouchables to their total ruin—the ruin which even the British had not perpetrated upon them. Their lands are forfeited for not paying the taxes in agitating against the government in a movemented by Moorthy.

A Brahmin, being the member of the highest caste, must think of highest things and happenings like marrying a princess as does Ramaswamy of *The Serpent and the Rope.* He must also practise and believe in vegetarianism and Yoga besides superior knowledge of the Vedas and Upanishads, the mainstay of Hinduism. However, he must display his indifference to worldly issues and possessions. This notion of overall superiority can be juxtaposed with a sense of glee, to the lower castes like warrior Nairs who amass wealth by loot and piracy. Their chief characteristic is reflected in their conduct of coercing everyone to offer bribes so that they can build their personal fortune on the misery of fellow countrymen. They are upwardly mobile by sending their children to English schools where they would learn to imitate foreign mannerisms and culture. This spirit of Brahminic denunciation of the lower castes resurfaces in Kirillov too who wants to be an anachronism: progressive and south Indian Brahmin both. In order to establish his claim to attention he would do anything - boast of his Brahminic origins, praise and condemn Gandhi and India by turns - with the sole aim of establishing his unmatchable dynamism.

# Kanthapura

*Kanthapura* (1938) is a small village in the Karwar district, high up in the Ghats on the Malabar Coast. It is situated on the banks of river Himavathi. Brahmins, potters, sudras, weavers and pariahs live in segregated quarters. All together there are twenty four houses in the Brahmin quarter and about a hundred huts in all the other quarters. Post-master Suryanarayan's house is the biggest among the Brahmins and Patel Range Gowda's nine-beamed one among the rest. Goddess Kenchamma is the presiding deity. The idol of Kanthapurishwari was dug up by Moorthy three years ago and consecrated by Bhatta and thus became the centre of the village life. Ramkrishnayya, the father of Rangamma, used to read out Sankara-Vijaya and Sastri would sing Harikathas. Money for these activities would be willingly donated by many and Moorthy would collect it in small sums from the majority as per their mite.

Moorthy, the only son of widow Narsamma, is a close follower of Mahatma Gandhi. He belongs to an orthodox Brahmin family, but he does not believe in untouchability and goes to the Pariahs and Sudras to collect donations for Harikathas and also to listen to their grievances. He has met Mahatma Gandhi in the city and has taken a vow to speak Truth, wear swadeshi and work for the upliftment of the downtrodden.

He devotes himself to the cause, sings the praise of Gandhi as the incarnation of God to liberate the suffering

Mother India and establishes the local Congress Committee after organizing the whole village except a few Brahmins with their interests vested in perpetuation of British rule. Among these are Bhatta who exploits the innocent village folks by advancing money on the security of land, Postmaster Suryanarayan, Patwari Nanjundia and the like. They see danger to themselves if the lower classes rise and learn to resist their exploitation by the Indian agents of the British. They resent a Brahmin's efforts to organize and educate the backward people. In collusion with the orthodox Swami in the city Bhatta, therefore, gets Moorthy excommunicated. Moorthy, however, is not affected and he does not bother about it. He continues to visit the sudras and pariahs and eats in their houses and holds classes for them. He also administers to them the vow of non-violence in the face of violence, truth and satyagraha as the aspects of their conduct.

When the news of Mahatma Gandhi's arrest reaches Kanthapura, therefore, he calls for action on the part of the members of Congress. All the pariahs, sudras and some Brahmins respond by picketing toddy-shops, violating toddy-groves, not paying revenue to the agents of the government. They are successful in winning over the coolies of Skeffington Coffee Estate to their side as against drinking toddy. They are mercilessly beaten all over the body, the woman's modesty violated and their private parts outraged. Several of them are killed in the firings. Moorthy is arrested and sentenced to three months in prison on the false charge of inciting the people to indulge in violence. But, the people do not lose courage and their protests continue despite repression let loose by the Red-man's government with the help of loyal agents like Bhatta, Swami, Patwari. When Moorthy is arrested the second time, Rangamma and in her absence Ratna come forward to lead the people in their satyagraha. Their lands are auctioned and punitive fines imposed on them but they refuse to be cowed down. Their women are raped, their houses ransacked and people killed indiscriminately by the police but they do not bow to accept defeat. Dispossessed of their lands and belongings, most of them leave Kanthapura and seek refuge with relatives, friends and sympathisers in Kashipura. The opportunists, however, take over the village and thrive imposed on them but they.

# The Serpent and the Rope

*The Serpent and the Rope* (1968) is the story of K Ramaswamy told autobiographically. He is the first and the only son of his mother who dies of asthama. His father marries and three daughters Kapila, Sukumari and Saroja are born to his stepmother who also dies. When Ramaswamy is twenty two his father marries the third time and dies leaving Sridhara, an eleven month old son to Vishalakshi, his last wife. He belongs to a very prosperous family of Brahmins, descendants of sage Yagnyavalkya, settled in Hyderabad. His grandfather Ramkrishnayya was distinguished for having an Eight-Pillared House and vast tracts of land and several buildings in and around Bangalore. Ramaswamy's father was a great mathematician and believed that the British would leave India only when shamed by Indians' superior scholarship. He was not sent to Europe for higher studies but Rama was sent to France to do research on the possible links between Bogomilitas and Druzes and thus search back for the Indian background—Jain or may be Buddhist—of the Cathars. (p. 15)

At the beginning of the story Ramaswamy has been in France wherefrom he comes to India to settle household and property affairs after the death of his father. He is already married to Madelein in France, five years his senior. Madelein has large properties in Aix-en-Provence and is employed as a teacher there. She loves Rama for his Brahmanism, vegetarianism and profound Vedic and Upanishadic scholarship. A son conceived after seven months of marriage is born to her in France while Ramaswamy is in India. She names her son Krishna, who dies in infancy. Madelein hates killing animals and believes in communism. Her parents died while she was quite young and is looked after by Oncle Charles. She is shy, innocent, very lovely—a Savoyan—and pure at heart. Her involvement with Rama is total and through association with him she becomes more and more immersed in Occidental occult sciences and ritual.

As the head of the family, Rama comes to solemnize his stepsister Saroja's marriage with a Delhi boy. Madelein is pregnant again. The second son too dies stillborn. This brings about a great change in the life and attitude of Madelein. She becomes more and more detached and resorts to Buddhist prayers, fasts and sadhana so much as to become a total stranger to Rama. He has to seek permission to enter her room. Madelein shies away from his touch even though for medicine and nursing. She acquires powers through meditation, yogasanas and the study of sacred texts. She observes fast for forty one days during which her prophecies come true at appointed times.

During his stay in France Ram develops asthamatic disease of lungs that keeps him mostly sick and convalescing. At the beginning Madelein nurses him to the best of her capacity like a truly devoted Indian wife. But the disease is a result more due to the climate of France that has not suited Ramaswamy. When he comes to attend Saroja's marriage, he falls sick and vomits blood and has to convalesce for months in Bangalore. But he has to go back to France to complete his research work. He has to write ten chapters to complete his thesis. Owing to this he has to visit several places in France as well as in England. Once, on his earlier visit to India, he had been introduced to Savithri, the daughter of an Indian prince of Surajpur. Savithri is sent to England and Rama has some very intimate moments—emotional, physical and spiritual—with her. By the time his research work nears completion, Madelein's detachment is also complete. She has no emotions left in her. Rising above the self, she seeks divorce from Rama so that he may go back to India a free man to marry an Indian woman. She does not want to spoil his chances of a fruitful life in India. France's climate has not suited him and she herself has become so withdrawn from the world itself. Ramaswamy is not too happy either. Being a Brahmin, he is unworldly in his attitude to his own pleasure, comforts and people. He is more devoted to scholarship than to individuals. His scholarly pursuits enlarge his vision in which he sees India as a Principle and himself and Madelein not as husband and wife but specks in the universe who act and yet are not motivated by any selfishness, pleasures or relations of the flesh. Born in the tradition of true Brahmins who are devoted to an understanding of the cosmos—Brahman—Ramaswamy sees the triumph of the higher religious virtues known as Catholicism.

Raja Rao's primary concern in *The Serpent and the Rope* is to establish the superiority of Indian thought of individual being a part of the universal. To interpret the complexities of the existence, there is no better guide than a true Brahmin devoted to scholarly pursuit of knowledge of the cosmos. A true Brahmin sees every individual, including himself, as a tiny particle clinging to the greater reality of God, separated from whom it may have no significance. The beauty of this exposition is that man learns to be so much detached even while immersed in worldly affairs head to foot. It trains him to believe and act to live not as a creator but as a puppet who may do all that it is capable of doing and yet may not be personally involved and may be recipient of material benefits—good or bad. Necessary jargon has been created to obtain the desired result and Raja Rao finds himself more and more bound to carry out this semblance. Ramaswamy says, "... I am not telling a story here, I am writing the sad and uneven chronicle of a life, my life, with no art or decoration, but with the "objectivity", the discipline of the "historical sciences", for by taste and tradition I am only a historian." (p. 231) Here he seems to have fallen in his own trap—so long as he tells the story of his own life, he is most unlikely to be 'objective'. Even if he were to go by what he says, there is still no reconciliation of his two opposite statements—that he is "writing the sad and uneven chronicle" of his life, is a statement of a person who claims to be above self. If he were above self, nothing would be 'sad' or 'uneven' to him. Since he attributes qualities to his job, he is admittedly being involved in value judgements.

# 'The Cat and Shakespeare': A Tale of India

*The Cat and Shakespeare* (1965) is the story of Govindan Nair, a clerk in the Rationing Office at Trivandrum. He lives next door to Ram Krishna Pai, a divisional clerk in the Revenue Board. Pai came only two years ago as a new appointee, after leaving his wife Saroja, daughter Usha aged 5, and son Vithal aged 3 at Pattanur. Pai lives in a small white house by the sea-side and eats his food at Home Friends. His wife's parents have thrived on piratic loot. That's why perhaps they have three-story houses at Alwaye. His natural worry is to send his children to English convents for better education besides providing them with a three-storey house to live in. Govindan Nair is a good conversationalist. He generally leaps across the boundary wall between their two houses, whenever he feels like talking to Pai.

Govindan Nair is primarily interested in amassing wealth, particularly mutli-storied houses and other luxury items. He is aware of his job in the ration office as a source of extra income. His hopes and calculations of wealth and property are based on the fact that every one needs a ration card for his food supplies during the famine years of War. But some people may need to draw excess rations. For a clerk in the ration office, it is not difficult to manipulate the actual requirements of the population of the district. To show exaggerated figures of foodgrains supplied and lost in transit and storage, are quite easy for a man like Govindan Nair. The official premium on a ration card in the black market is two rupees. At this rate of income Nair feels happy to realize that he could have a three-story house—quite a symbol of status and wealth in Trivandrum where even cousins of kings like Raja Raja Rajendra Verma had only two-storey houses.

Lots of black money is generated during the War. In this game every one thrives. If the bosses don't connive, the assistants cannot indulge corruption. But, in the ration office and the revenue board office nothing moves or happens without money exchanging hands. Bogus ration cards are issued and the record is shown destroyed by rats or simply missing. This is how the boss John built a decent house to himself. Govindan Nair contracts to buy the house in which Ram Krishna Pai lives, from its owner Murugan Mudali for seventeen thousand rupees. Mudali was a toddy tapper who prospered by black-marketing during the War. Govindan Nair buys the house in the name of Ram Krishna's daughter Usha who is selected to marry Sridhar, the only son of Govindan Nair. The first instalment of seven thousand is paid by Ram Krishna Pai from the horde of Govindan Nair kept in his custody.

Shridhar soon dies and Usha keeps living with Ram Krishna Pai. He has been in love with Shantha, a teacher in the Nair Society High School. Shantha is pregnant. Soon Govindan Nair is arrested for accepting bribe of one hundred and nine rupees from a lady in Vulzehvanoor. Her son had a ration shop and he had grown very rich very fast. When Govindan Nair reaches his office, he finds a cat put in a cage on the table. This is the doing of John. Govindan discovers that a confidential inquiry has been ordered into the disappearance of seventeen bags of rice in transit and also how the movement of foodgrains came to be known to public. The case is first tried and Govindan argues in his defence. He has studied law for a year. But his cock-and-bull story type of defence does not help him and he is convicted.

After his release from jail he pays the second instalment of seven thousand rupees to Mudali and spends three thousand for buying ornaments for Usha and Shantha. He remains unaffected by whatever has happened and is transferred to Alwaye. Ram Krishna Pai is promoted Secretary of Temple Grants Department at the Revenue Board.

An earlier version of *The Cat and Shakespeare* appeared under the title of the Cat in Chelsen Review Summer, 1959. The narrative of *The Cat and Shakespeare* employs the imageries of mother-cat and Shakespearen drama running parallel to each other. The imagery of mother-cat has been employed central to the theme of corruption flourishing not in isolation but under hierarchical patronage. The Ration-office during the war-days of scarcity and Revenue office are places were illegal premium dictates priorities and expedites disposal of public demands. Since the above two departments deal in matters of vital importance affecting one and all, there is a lot of scope for bribery and black marketing. In fact, the rates of bribery have come to be acknowledged for different items and the clerks and supervisors have not much to talk about except calculations of wealth and property amassable by those working in these offices. The higher official knows the items and areas which allow inflow of extra income to the subordinate. This is perhaps because he himself had at some time worked in the lower post and also because he derives his own income by corrupt means. It does not pay to disturb the lower one in pursuing his income on the principle of not throwing stones at others by those living in glass houses. As a matter of fact, it is the duty of the higher one to oversee the indulgence of the lower one in a patronizing way in the manner of the mother cat. Whenever the mother cat senses some danger to its kittens, it springs from nowhere and lifts the kittens by neck to safety. To the onlooker it may appear very cruel and dangerous for the kitten to be lifted by neck as the carnivore kills its prey by crushing the windpipe and blood-pipe that is vulnerable most in the throat. But the cat that kills the mice by seizing the neck, does not intend to act the same way in the case of its kitten. Though the kitten dangling by neck between the cat's teeth do look no different from the mouse preyed upon, there is a qualitative difference between the two approaches of the cat on two different occasions. In the former case it discharges the duty of a guardian who has not only to protect its progeny from the impending harm but also to ensure their efficient learning of the art of hunting their prey. The mother cat appears on the scene only when she senses danger and removes its kitten to a safer place which she alone knows and decides. This cannot be easily appreciated by the onlooker.

The other aspect of the personality of a cat is that it is fond of milk. While it drinks milk, however, it shuts its vision to forget existence of the whole world behind it. May be it denotes the cat's love of the best pleasures of life in complete disregard of the possible dangers and once it is able to get at them, it tends to ignore the possible dangers that attend upon the theft of such pleasures.

Govindan Nair's indulgence in corruption and his consequent conviction can be interpreted in the light of the above two aspects. Raja Rao subtitles the story as "A Tale of Modern India." The dominant theme of the narrative is bureaucratic corruption that is the gift of the so called progressive system of British outlook and administration. How petty officials thrive on human misery and undermine the foundations of a society in peril, has seized the imagination of the writer. There are adequate references to the banditry, thuggery, piracy upon which foundations of family business and reputation are built. This is what exactly the British as successful merchants are proud of. Their efforts are backed by their intelligentsia and their imperialism is justified not only by their vested interests but also by their artists, writers and thinkers. It is thus in this context that the importance of Shakespeare can be underlined. Shakespeare has enjoyed greater love and prestige in India than in his native England. He is treated as the greatest dramatist, poet and wise man for all times to come. This is the scene in India where he is studied with more devotion than understanding. There is more imitation than integration of scholarship and wisdom so far as Shakespeare is concerned. He is criticised more at home. However, Shakespeare and the British system of administration are complementary to each other. Raja Rao seems to suggest that Shakespeare and corruption are the two most charming gifts of the British to India. These are the two myths that sustain each in perpetuation.

# 'Comrade Kirillov'

Kirillov is the assumed name of an Indian from an orthodox Brahmin family of Adyar in the South. He reaches California, USA to study religious philosophy in the context of the world at large and be an Indian messiah showing the right path to the world. He is learned and a brilliant intellectual. He is honest and frugal in his habits and diet. Though he belongs to a rich family with big lands and twelve-pillared house owing to their loyalty to the English, Kirillov finds English presence undesirable on Indian soil. He becomes interested in socialism and learns German and French in order to be able to read and understand works of Karl Marx, Engels, Fourier and Saint Simons—the prominent philosophers of socialism. He is encouraged to study Russian so that he can understand Lenin, the messiah of the working class people. He also decides to leave America for London as a right stepping-stone. He travels second class on ship and reaches Liverpool with very little baggage and lodges in a dingy room of a Greek Street hotel. Here he meets members of Labour Party and becomes interested in its programme. His friends Patlock or Peter Ree would keep him most of the company. They were interested in India and had studied Mahatma Gandhi. In London Raja Rao is taken to see him as a reporter for *The Hindu*. Raja Rao himself has been on a mission of collecting signatures on an appeal against Moscow trials. He discovers Kirillov is his distant cousin. Raja Rao is scared after the reports of Nuremberg trials and has come to believe more and more in Gandhian philosophy. However, he finds Kirillov alienated from Gandhi after his obsession with Marx. He finds the pro-Capitalist atmosphere of London wicked because it tends to lead an India-sympathiser away from seeking basic and radical solutions in preference over the crumbs the Englishmen would like to offer. He also realizes the tricky nature of the British Museum setup which is not conducive to worthwhile research and that soaks all the energy one has. Raja Rao finds him busy with the new book under contemplation for the last six years to be titled, "Mahatma Gandhi—A Marxian Interpretation." Kirillov believes non-violence to be biological lie and Gandhi an ungrown adult mystic and 'Kleptomaniac'. For Kirillov, the answer to the ills of India is the establishment of a classless society where master-servant relationship will be extinct. He also criticises Gandhi for his peaceful methods of attaining freedom from the British. Kirillov refuses to sign the petition calling parliamentary democracy a hypocrisy incapable of solving any of the human problems.

The second part of the narrative opens in 1948, with the author reminiscing about Kirillov. He has married a Polish national Irene. She is a loving wife, a good host, a nurse and a card holding member of the Communist Party. The War is on and international marriages are officially welcome in London which has come to stand for Freedom and Liberty. India has declared support for English war efforts. Stalin too has aligned with Britain against Hitler. Communists, so far suspected and discriminated against, become respectable. Kirillov feels inspired and writes an astonishing thesis incorporating labour theories on the people's war and calls it 'India and Our Struggle.' Meanwhile politics takes an about turn in India and with the launching of 'Quit India' movement prospects change in favour of Gandhi. A son is born to Kirillov-Irene and is named Kamal instead of Stephanovich as decided before birth. Irene and Kamal learn Hindustani language and culture and are well-versed in Sanskrit literature. Kirillov has visited India after twenty five years of arrival and has met his brothers prospering as Congressmen. He has had darshana of Ramana Maharishi of Tiruvanamala and Nehru. He finds nothing wrong with Pakistan and Muslims who killed only on the instigation of their British commanders. He also finds Islam more progressive than Hinduism and Muslim masses of Bombay, Ahmedabad, Calcutta and Cownpore most progressive force.

The last part is in the form of Irene's diary which records her anguish over Stalin's congratulations to Hitler for having won Poland. She loves to be an Indian because an Indian is basically a Sadhu. Kirillov cannot bear to hear anybody denouncing India or Gandhi and has come to hate Europe. The dairy also records his impressions of deep hatred and distrust between Hindus and Muslims. The final commentary is made by Raja Rao in the person of a reporter of *The Hindu* in which he describes the myth of how Kanyakumari came to be called as such after Lord Shiva's failure to turn up to wed Parvati waiting at the last rock at the tip of India into the ocean.

## 'The Chessmaster and His Moves'

*The Chessmaster and His Moves* (1988) is the story of Ramaswamy-Madeleine - Savithri retold in an enlarged form of more than 700 pages. Its protagonist is Sivarama Sastri, a Tamil brahmin, Suzanna, a spiritually inclined French actress, Jayalaskshmi, a sick North Indian traditional woman of princely stock. Here again is an attempt to establish the superiority of Indian belief and conduct and the misery of the Indian hero left high and dry in the west. The locale is Paris. This time Mireille indulges adultery, instead of Laxmi of *The Serpent and the Rope*, and the surgery is performed to remove a cyst from J.'s brain to recall Ramaswamy's lung operation from the earlier novel. Even the teacher-pupil dialogues are in the same vein of upholding the hero's point of view alone: "I was not interested in going out to prove anything to any one. I wanted to prove everything to myself."

The Chessmaster is eternal Siva. He does not take responsibility for any activity and indulges eating, sleeping, defecating and sex. Arrangements for the stay and treatment of Uma in Paris are made by friends. Suzanne is one single source of all supplies—cooked food, clean kitchenette, nurses him in sickness, takes care of his mail and even offer her body. But Siva appreciates only by complaining against her desire for a child. He finds living with her dry and melancholic. Siva does not find anything objectionable in incestuous attachment to sister Jean-Pierre and Mireille. Raja Ashok and Jaya are all behaving that way. This seems to echo the marriage between cousins considered preferential in the South India.

*The Chessmaster and His Moves* is, thus, one more massive attempt to recreate a world lost and distorted by myths. Everything in this novel belongs to the past—Victorian, to be more precise. Indian middle class in love with foreign cars, domestic servants of a variety of races; rushing to foreign countries for treatment of common maladies; dancing girls providing an important engagement; love and display of silks and jewelleries; sojourns in Europe and children's upbringing in Europian institutions. The extra-marital courting by partners in India makes it a scene borrowed from the French licentious society. However, deep beneath these superficially camouflaged intents seems lurking an attempt to explore the atman-parmatman (individual soul-Supreme Being) relationship. The whole of the text is replete with the call to merge the self with the Higher Consciousness. There is no place for ego borne on worldly considerations like family relationships, wealth, position and so on. One should act as if he or she were doing it as a matter of call of duty. What is important today in one position may not be so tomorrow or in another situation. The novel emphasises upon the raising of the spiritual and intellectual level where the temporal and the animal loses its significance. It subverts and ridicules the human tendency to ignore the need for a vision of an elated existence henceforth promoted by a will to surrender to the fictitious charms of the past. The past accounts are all the result of indulgence in fancy. The harsher realities and cruder sufferings are rarely included in the transformed version of the past happenings. The strongest evidence of it is available in myths. A simple attempt to deconstruct them would render vast data that would disillusion the egotistic mortal and convince him of his being a mere chess-piece on the Universal board, moved by the Grand Chessmaster.

## 'On the Ganga Ghat'

*On the Ganga Ghat* (1993) is a series of short stories written in a sequence to form a novel. The first episode records the arrival and presence of all types of people from all corners of the land in Benares. Everyone who arrives expects to be received royally but soon gets lost in meditating the mysteries of existence and coincidents. Distances and differences become meaningless and merge into each other in the face of the reality of death on the banks of the Ganga. This way alone one can expect to earn merit. A whiteman Paul alongwith Raja Rao arrives in Benaras with the expectation of experiencing the Vedic times through Sanskrit chantings everywhere. There is Bhim - Rupvati, the parrot couple living for very long on a tree along the Dashashwamedh Ghat, the ultimate destiny of the pious on earth. They are considered Prabhavati a queen reborn with her maid in attendance. Their appearance and feeding is a divine act not witnessed by everyone. Equally divine is the disappearance of Bhim who sacrificed itself on the funeral pyre of the most accomplished Siddheshwarji.

The primary aim of all those who come to Benaras is to earn merit by dying there. This is well known to the crematorium attendant, the pyre-wood seller. Even the curs and vultures know it and each one of them tries to pay tribute to the departed soul and to the bereaved as per his nature of profession and being. All those who dominate the scene are the Brahmins, the crematoria personnel, the widows and the bier bearers. Each one is busy doing justice to his job by taking it full-size because death is the ultimate reality. It becomes meritorious in the sanctified and religiously surcharged atmosphere of Benaras.

It is certain that people are drawn towards Benaras mostly after reaching a turning point in their grief-stricken consciousness. They may do business like Muthradas or may be a devout Muslim in the service of their Hindu masters, like Muhammad but each one of them tends towards piety after undergoing the pangs of some moral wrong or curse. Such people are simple credulous folks unconcerned with the depths of philosophical statements like awakening and dreaming and sleeping, even though they read holy books of knowledge and speak the language open to mysterious interpretations. But each one waits for the ultimate howsoever he comprehends it.

Where throng the devout, there would abound the occultists too. Astrologers reading and preparing horoscopes and predicting future of individuals are in great demand in Benaras. The phenomenon includes children's birth, their marriage and begetting of grand sons, for the latter are essential for a Hindu to attain salvation. Shankar, the astrologer's son, therefore, has one important prayer to mother Ganga asking for the birth of a son to perpetuate the lineage. However, the would-be father desires a son not interested in sins and vices like boozing, womanising and smoking. Those humble like Bhola from Rajgarh, who have been on war expedition to Europe, come to Benaras with their whole family to pay obeisance to mother Ganga and never go back after losing everyone near and dear. For, the Ganga consoles the inconsolable and draws the rudderless to her breast. This contention is reinforced in the tragic tale of Rani Rasomani, the queen of the Raja of Bankipur. Whereas every other woman has children, Rasomani does not beget even one, that too in spite of seeking the blessings of saints and astrologers' talismans. However, her husband dies before they start on their pilgrimage to Prayag and Benaras. This is indicative of the strong belief that mother Ganga would not let anyone go without fulfilment. Rasomani, therefore, visits Benaras never to return after discovering that she is pregnant! The eternal Benaras is the dead-end of all life and its chatter. It does neither look back or connect with the distant. It is its own universe and frowns at the temporal. The material world cannot lure one back to its fold. One becomes indifferent to titles, wealth and even lineage here.

This aversion to money and possessions is clearly demonstrated in the episode of Shiv, who had seen his mother being driven out after disgrace to his father by his uncle. Shiv had vowed to avenge it and made lots of money to fulfil his mission. He volunteers to become a pimp to a concubine and forsakes everything after coming under the influence of a Sadhu. He even tears to pieces the currency notes he had amassed because during the course of his long association with Ganga he rises above all mean ideas and missions. Benaras, the abode of all the degenerate, sufferers and sinners brings about a transformation in the whole personality of man. Prostitutes and concubines, murderers and usurpers, all tend towards purity of soul and indifference to worldly possessions. The experience of Ranchoddoss is in tune with the above observation too. A man of integrity in jewellery business in Bombay, his doted daughter Sudha displays signs of total indifference towards worldly charms and desires even in her youth. She chants and meditates on God and observes fasts. She has the premonition that a Sadhu is her destiny from her preceding birth in Kathiawad. When a handsome Sadhu Sunderanandji visits the household, she is given a farewell by the family. Later, Ranchoddoss too migrates to Benaras after his wife's death and marriage of his sons. He finds Sudha offering a discourse on deeper philosophy of life, soul and the Supreme Being. She is at supreme peace with herself, to the great elation of her father. All this is the effect of the presence of divine Ganga. However, the priests have fabricated so many complications that confuse the people instead of enlightening them and making their existence a delightful internal experience.

*On the Ganga Ghat* is a beautiful chain of discourses in the gossip mode. Its effectiveness lies in the simplicity with which the inexplicable mysteries of life have been explained. Though, on the superficial plane, it appears that the writer's imagination is bogged down in contradictory instances brought to the fore, this juxtaposition goes down deep well for it allows the reader to see through the fog of fanciful mythologisation indulged in over ages. It very precisely conveys that the holiness of a place permeates the life-styles, needs and attitudes of the visitor and encourages him to embrace the positive and better option of life. Despite the presence of so many vice-generating factors, even the evil and the vice lose their as a cobra becomes harmless after emptying itself of the accumulated venom. The vested interests like Mumbo-jumbo chanting priests, sex-chasers and last-riters are all helpless victims of the demands of material existence and would seek no encouragement or approval from any other agent to renounce or modify their indulgences. This contributes to and strengthens the belief that the Ganga is not just flowing waters but a circular movement that is capable of churning the vice out of itself. It does not get polluted in spite of receiving all the filth of the whole worldly systems, and offers a message that the external factors cannot change the basic nature of existence. The superficial can coverup the genuine for a little while but will get thrown out sooner or later, provided the inclination within is not crushed or suppressed. If seemingly neutral waters can cause so much transformation in the psyche of man and lead him to the positive ways, then hope will survive and regenerate itself and peace of mind and soul will be attained. The thrust of his rhetoric is to establish that Benaras is a place full of anecdotes, mythological fables and actual happenings, all of which purport to strengthen the message that everyone, whether noble or evil, tends to indulge piety. The source of this piety is the motherly Ganga that is source of all life and its activity. The Ganga inspires as well as regulates and salvages soul.

# Bibliography

*Kanthapura*. London: George Allen and Unwin, 1938,

Indian edn. Bombay: Oxford University Press. Champak Library, 1947.

*The Cow of the Barricades and Other Stories:* Bombay: Oxford Univ. Press, Champak Library, 1947.

*The Serpent and the Rope:* Bombay: John Murray, 1960, Indian edn. New Delhi: Hind Pocket Books, 1968.

*The Cat and Shakespeare: A Tale of Modern India.* New York: Macmillan, 1965, Ind. Edn., New Delhi: Hind Pocket Books, 1971.

*Comrade Kirillov.* New Delhi: Orient Paperback, 1976.

*The Policeman and the Rose.* New Delhi: Oxford Univ. Press, 1978.

*The Chessmaster and His Moves.* New Delhi: Vision Books, 1988.

*On the Ganga Ghat.* New Delhi: Vision Books, 1989.

**Secondary Sources**

Naik, M.K. *Raja Rao,* New York, Twayne, 1972.

Narasimhaiah, C.D. *Raja Rao.* New Delhi: Arnold Heinemann, 1973.

Niven, Alastair. *Truth Within Fiction: A Study of Raja Rao's Serpent and the Rope.* Calcutta: Writers Workshop, 1978.

Rao, K.R *The Fiction of Raja Rao,* Aurangabad: Parimal Prakashan, 1980.

Sharma, J.P. *Raja Rao: A Visionary in Indo-Anglian Fiction.* Meerut: Shalabh, 1980.

Sharma, K.K. *ed. Perspectives on Raja Rao.* Ghaziabad: Vimal Prakashan, 1980.

Alam, Qaiser Zoha. "Kanthapura's Style: A Point of View," *Language Forum,* Vol. V, No. 2, July-Sept. 1979.

Ali, Ahmad. "Illusion and Reality: The art and philosophy of Raja Rao," *The Journal of Commonwealth Literature,* No. 5, July 1968.

Amur, G.S. "Raja Rao: The Kannada Phase," *The Journal of Karnataka University,* Vol. X, Humanities, 1966.

Anjaneyulu, D. *"The Cat and Shakespeare:* A Tale of Modern India," *Thought,* New Delhi, Feb. 5, 1966.

Dey, Esha. "A Baroque Stylization: A Note on Raja Rao's *The Serpent and Rope," Language Forum,* New Delhi, Vol. VI, No. 3, Oct.-Dec. 1980.

———, "Fissures in being: Anguish and Alienation in *The Serpent and the Rope," Littcrit,* University of Kerala, Trivandrum, July, 1981.

———, "India: The Thematic Axis of Raja Rao' *Comrade Kirillov, An* Antinovel," *Commonwealth Quarterly,* The Centre for Commonwealth Literature and Research, University of Mysore, September 1981.

Eng, Oil Boo. "Making Initial Innocent Sense of *The Serpent and the Rope," The Journal of Indian Writing in English,* Dept. of English, Annamali University, Annamalainagar, Vol. 8, Jan-Jul. 1980.

Fremonth-Smith, Eliot. "Proverb hunting in Paradox Land," *The New York Times,* Jan. 20, 1965.

Gemill, Janet Powers. "Rhythm in *The Cat and Shakespeare," Literature East and West,* Vol. xiii, I & II, 1969.

Harrex, S.C. "The Fascination of What is Difficult: Some Student Responses to Raja Rao," K.K. Sharma, ed., *Indo-English Literature,* Ghaziabad: Vimal Prakashan, 1977.

Hartley Lois. "The Serpent and the Rope," *America* CVIA, May 4, 1963.

Iyengar, K.R.S. "Literature as Sadhana," *Aryan Path*, Vol. 40, Nos. 6-7, June-July 1969.

Mukherjee, Meenakshi. "Raja Rao's Shorter Fiction," *Indian Literature*, Vol. X, No. 3, 1967.

Nagarajan, S. "An Indian Novel: A Review of *The Serpent and the Rope*," *The Sewanee Review*, Summer, 1964.

Naik, M.K. "*Kanthapura:* The Anglo-Indian Novel as Legendary History," *The Journal of Karnataka University*, Vol. X, 1966.

———, "The Serpent and the Rope; the Indo-Anglian Novel as Epic Legend," in M.K. Naik, G.S. Amur and S.K. Desai, (ed). *Critical Essays on Indian Writing in English*, Dharwar: Karnatak University, 1968.

———, "The Achievement of Raja Rao," *The Banasthali Patrika*, Rajasthan, No. 12, Jan. 1969.

———, "The Kingdom of God is within a Mew: A Study of *The Cat and Shakespeare*," *The Journal of Karnataka University*, Vol. Xiii, Humanities, 1968.

Narsimhaiah, C.D. "National Identity in Literature and Language: Its Range and Depth in the Novels of Raja Rao," *National Identity*, ed. K.L. Goodwin, London: Heinemann, 1970.

———, "Raja Rao: The Metaphysical Novel *(The Serpent and the Rope)* and Its Significance for Our Age," *Readings in Commonwealth Literature*, ed. William Walsh, Oxford: Clarendon Press, 1973.

Natwar-Singh, K. "Return Passage to India." *Saturday Review*, March 16, 1963.

Patil, B. Chandrashekhar. "The Kannada Element in Raja Rao's Prose: A Linguistic Study of Kanthapura," *The Journal of Karnataka University*, Vol. XIII, 1969.

Prescott, Orville. "The Serpent and the Rope," *New York Times*, Feb. 22, 1963.

Raizada, Harish. "Literature as Sadhana: The Progress of Raja Rao from *Kanthapura* to *The Serpent and the Rope*," K.K. Sharma, ed. *Indo-English Literature*.

Rao, J.S. "Concepts of Times and Death in Raja Rao's *The Cat and Shakespeare*," *Littcrit*, University of Kerala, Vol. 2, No. 2, Dec. 1976.

Ray, Robert J. "The Novels of Raja Rao," *Books Abroad*, Oklahama Univ., Autumn 1966.

Sastry, L.S.R. Krishna. "Raja Rao," *Triveni*, Madras, Jan. 1968.

Shahane, V.A. "Raja Rao's *The Cat and Shakespeare*: A Study in the Form of Fiction," *The Journal of Indian Writing in English*, Vol. 3, No. 1, Jan. 1975.

Sharma, Atma Ram. "Peasant Sensibility in *Kanthapura*," K.K. Sharma, ed., *Indo-English Literature*.

———, "Raja Rao: Cats, Serpents, Comrades and of Human Condition," *Perspective*, Calcutta, May, 1978.

Shepherd, R. "Symbolism in *The Cat and Shakespeare*," *World Literature Written in English, Commonwealth General Journal*, XIV, 1975.

Taranath, Rajeev. "A Note on the Problem of Simplification in Raja Rao's *The Serpent and the Rope*," *Fiction and the Reading Public*, ed. C.D. Narasimhaiah, Mysore: The University of Mysore, 1967.

Thakur, Guruprasad. "Reflections on Rama. India as Depicted in *The Serpent and the Rope*." *The Journal of Indian Writing in English*, Vol. 2, No. 2, July 1974.

Tucker, Martin. "Cultures in Conflict," *The Commonwealth*, Jan. 25, 1965.

Zuckerman, Ruth Van Hart. "The Cat and Shakespeare," *Books Abroad*, Summer 1965.

# Index

K



L

M

R



S

**T**

□□□